DWARF ⚳ PLANET
A PRACTICAL GUIDE THROUGH DEPRESSION

BENJAMIN SLEDGE

ISBN: 978-0-9991545-2-6

Layout and graphic design by HeartSupport, Inc.

HeartSupport, Inc.
PO Box 19461
Austin, TX 78760
info@heartsupport.com
www.heartsupport.com

To my fellow veterans,
who often return home from a strange land,
only to fight a new war on a different planet

CONTENTS

INTRØDUCTIØN

My good friend Andre Bradford wrote a poem about depression a few years ago. A champion slam poet, he's a deep thinker and wields words like a samurai with a sword. What I didn't know up until that point was how much he'd struggled with depression. Upon hearing his poem—entitled "Dwarf Planet"—I knew he had discovered a key to unlock a conversation many people aren't having.

Around us, the mental health crisis rages. Many of the people we meet day-to-day who appear happy and well adjusted are screaming internally. They feel cold, out of orbit, and stranded. Whether in politics, at our churches, within friend groups, or across social media, we know there's a deep need for mental health resources. While the stigma has been lifted to a degree, the resources for help are limited.

HeartSupport—the nonprofit organization that produced this workbook (and to which all proceeds go)—works directly in the hard rock and metal music industry providing fans the resources they need. Our founder Jake Luhrs of the Grammy-nominated metal band August Burns Red can tell you story after story of men and women begging him for help. Just anything to ease their affliction. A lot of nonprofit social services and mental health entities have a tendency to raise awareness or give proceeds to mental health facilities. But what about the people looking for something now? What about those who could use a resource to take steps to reclaim their life? Jake decided to step into that space and have HeartSupport be the entity that creates workbooks and programs people could use as opposed to deflecting to other sources.

When we polled our audience at HeartSupport, we were shocked to find that over 60 percent struggled with depression. The problem we ran into, however, was how to tackle the elephant in the room. Even with the stigma around depression, it was still the least pressing of the issues regarding mental health. What we discovered, however, was that depression is the most urgent challenge and often a contributor to other problems within our society.

After consulting Dr. Michelle Saari, our mental health advisor, we found the data were there to back us up. We surveyed 500 men and women battling through depression and asked them to give us personal insight that many people will find new and enlightening and hopefully provide a fresh outlook on depression. Armed with Andre's key to unlock the conversation, the information to rattle the foundations, and a drive to kick in the door, we began the long trek to explore the barren wasteland known as depression. The result of years of coaching, studying, victories, failures, and personal experience is what you hold in your hands.

The ship is leaving the dock, and we're hell bent on helping men and women find their way off the dwarf planet.

We hope and pray this workbook is the escape pod you've been looking for.

♇

HOW TO USE THIS WORKBOOK

—

When we see actor Chris Evans on the big screen, we would never guess he was battling through deeper existential questions or facing down depression and anxiety. We only see the impeccable character of Captain America.

Yet in a recent online interview, Evans revealed his lifelong battle with depression and social anxiety. While many of us admire him for his iconic role as Captain America, what most people don't know is that he turned down the role on four separate occasions. He admitted that the thought of becoming a big-name actor and losing control over his personal freedoms caused intense anxiety, leading to bouts of depression. He wasn't sure if he wanted to be known only for his superhero roles. What if a family member got sick and while visiting the hospital people only wanted to take photos of him because he's a celebrity? He ended up seeing a therapist before he took the role to process everything he was facing.

Being a superhero is all part of the script. When Chris is offstage, life isn't scripted, and he doesn't have superpowers. He's human, like you and me, and the chaotic nature of life can easily cause distractions.

So what was Chris's advice at the end of the interview to those watching? Show up daily. Be present in life. Quiet your mind and explore the emotions and problems you're facing.

It's a bit harder when there's no script, and this [life] is just happening in a chaotic form, but the hunt for the moment—the hunt to be present—that's the goal. My goal in life is to be present.

And it's hard.
—CHRIS EVANS

This workbook isn't a script for a better life—because if it were, you'd know the ending just like movie stars know the endings before the audience does. Instead, think of this workbook as a guide to exploring the unknowns in depression while discovering your own answers along the way.

Like an astronaut exploring the mysteries of the cosmos, you'll come to discover new and revealing facts you haven't known before about your depression. You'll step into worlds you weren't even aware existed and seek new ways to navigate the terrain of depression.

But here's the catch.

Just like Chris Evans advised, you have to show up and be present. And that will be hard. At times, going through the exercises may seem overwhelming. You must explore areas you claimed you wouldn't revisit to get the full picture. But if you show up each day, engage in the content, and move forward through the exercises, you'll be surprised how much you learn about yourself and new ways to navigate depression.

So now the ask: Can you do that? If so, let's start by committing to this process.

MY NAME IS

AND I AM COMMITTED TO EXPLORING MY STORY OF DEPRESSION THROUGHOUT THIS WORKBOOK.

YOUR SIGNATURE

THE DWARF PLANET

CHAPTER 1

As a teenager, I found that one of the easiest test questions in science class was to name the nine planets in our solar system: Mercury, Venus, Earth, Mars, Jupiter, Saturn, Uranus, Neptune, and Pluto.

Only Pluto isn't a planet anymore. In 2006, the International Astronomical Union reclassified it as a "dwarf planet." While Pluto followed the same patterns as other planets—orbiting around the sun and spherical in shape—it wasn't gravitationally dominant. So with the swipe of a pen, Pluto disappeared from textbooks and tests. Sometimes the dwarf planet became a trick question to throw off students about the number of planets in our solar system.

The backlash was fierce initially as the internet took up arms and fashioned the latest memes. The joke became, "When I was your age, Pluto was a planet." But over time, people accepted the loss of our ninth and exiled planet where it has remained frozen, barren, and lifeless.

One thing I discovered common across the board for men and women struggling through depression was how similar our conditions were to that of the now-alienated planet Pluto.

When my wife, Emily, entered her freshman year in college at the University of Texas, she found the next three years of her life marked by intense depression. While she had amazing friends and made good grades, many days she could barely pull herself out of bed to go to class or find the energy to interact with others.

I, myself, had a different experience with depression when I returned home from war.

Today there are still misconceptions about depression: *People are just sad and they'll get over it. Depression isn't a real mental health issue. It's just a fad.* Others dismiss depression as a minor mental health ailment, not worthy of any real attention as a major issue facing society. They downgrade it to dwarf planet status.

But for those suffering from depression, the experience is real. One person told us in the survey:

> **Depression is like being stuck in a dark, cold trench all alone. It feels impossible to get out of, like all you've known is the darkness and that's all you'll ever know. Then people parade around above you where the sun shines on their backs and they say things like, "I can see it's bad in there. At least you won't get sunburned!" All you can try to do is see past enough of the darkness to find your footing and get up every morning.**

Kinda sounds like Pluto doesn't it?

With depression, you're in a cold, lifeless place, and you're on the fringes of the solar system all alone. Sure, you can see the sun from afar and know other people are having the time of their life, but you're stuck on this dwarf planet of an illness no one cares about.

While Pluto sat waiting to be discovered until 1930, scientists estimate it's been around for over four billion years. Just like Pluto, *depression* is a fairly new term. Its description is often loose in today's vocabulary, so people have trouble identifying just what it is. But what most don't know is that records of depression have existed since ancient times.

DEPRESSIØN THRØUGH THE AGES

A rose by any other name would smell as sweet.
—ROMEO & JULIET

In Shakespeare's play about tragically fated lovers, Romeo and Juliet, Juliet makes a point that regardless of the name, a rose is still a rose. We could call depression something else, but the symptoms would still identify it as depression.

In the same vein, depression's original label—melancholia—first appeared in ancient Mesopotamian texts. Throughout history, documents recorded by shamans, healers, monks, priests, philosophers, and writers give us varying degrees of depression's effects.

I'll spare you a long and boring history lesson and instead paint this picture. Imagine for a moment you're bitten by an animal in ancient Egypt that causes your life-span to extend to 8,000 years. The catch is that the infection from the bite also causes severe depression. Desperate to understand the cause and find a cure, you visit with the priests and shamans in your town. They're convinced it's a demon or evil spirit and try an exorcism. It doesn't work so they try beatings and starvation.

Not wanting to endure the abuse any longer, you wait a few thousand years until medicine advances and migrate to ancient Greece. The physicians recommend physical and mental exercises. So you do gymnastics, have musicians dressed up as centaurs, play the flute to brighten your mood, take baths, and sometimes indulge in opiates they prescribe. Sometimes you go on a diet.

Throughout the millennia, you sometimes get locked up in an insane asylum. Sometimes they try bloodletting (a process of making a cut to let "bad" blood drain out), and other times you are thought to have endured past grief and trauma that's causing your depression.

At the turn of the twenty-first century psychologists claim depression is chemical or mental. Others say it's a lack of direction and purpose or inability to construct a future. Some ask you to try electroshock therapy. Others claim you suffer from the stress of living 8,000 years.

I give you this hypothetical scenario to show you how people have diagnosed depression since antiquity and how physicians have treated the condition throughout the ages. From ancient Greece, to medieval Europe, to the Enlightenment, to our modern era, depression has been documented and treated in a myriad of ways (some of which are downright bizarre and disturbing). Some techniques have worked for people. Other times they've had disastrous results.

One thing is certain, however. Throughout thousands of years, we've seen depression play a role in humanity—with many causes and in many forms.

THE MANY FORMS OF DEPRESSION

If you were to search online for an image of a depressed person, there's a good chance you'd find a picture of someone looking sad or mopey. Maybe their head's hung low or they look tired.

To many, that's how we'd stereotype what a depressed person looks like. However, several people who report depression are productive and outgoing. On the exterior, you'd never label them sad or mopey.

But internally? What's really going on inside a person? That varies drastically.

When I started researching depression, I wanted to hear from numerous men and women who suffered under its weight. The team at HeartSupport was looking for answers from real people who wanted to take part, not just statistics reported by a data center. So we surveyed 500 willing participants living with depression to see what we could learn. When we asked them to describe what depression felt like, their answers varied greatly. What was fascinating after reviewing the results was that common themes and similarities emerged.

The most common sensation people described was like an actual weight they were carrying or that something was pressing down on them. They explained that this feeling led to other negative side effects that other people reported. One respondent shared the following:

> *Depression is the feeling of holding a brick in your chest. Sometimes it hurts so much that it crushes the air right out of you. It makes it harder to get out of bed, to get your groceries, to do everything in your day. There's nothing that will expel this brick from your body, so any hobby, passion, or outlet loses its appeal. Without a release or a passion, you lose your purpose, comfort, and passions; you essentially lose anything that makes you, well, you. After carrying that brick around for days, weeks, and months, it accumulates weight. Rock bottom is when the brick has crushed your heart, your lungs, your stomach, and your desire to live. You don't eat. You don't sleep or you sleep too much. You don't move because you can't carry the brick one step further. You're paralyzed and stripped of your identity as the days pile up and it seems like there's no end in sight.*

Of the people we surveyed, many responded they felt numb, empty, hollow, or tired. Others felt as if they were drowning or enveloped in a thick fog or wet blanket. Still others described being a zombie who felt hopeless and without motivation, direction, or purpose.

Why does any of this matter?

You may feel as if you're the only one in the world feeling the way you do. You may even feel shame thinking your depression "isn't normal." One thing that has helped hundreds of people at our organization—heartsupport.com—is by discovering they're not the only one going through something. They meet hundreds of other men and women who say, "Yeah, I deal with the same thing."

So how common is depression and what you're dealing with? Let's look at just how many men and women understand what you're going through.

 **35.5%** COLLEGE STUDENTS WHO SAID THEY "FELT SO DEPRESSED THAT IT WAS DIFFICULT TO FUNCTION."

THE NUMBER OF WOMEN WHO ARE MORE LIKELY THAN MEN TO EXPERIENCE DEPRESSION IN THEIR LIFETIME. **70%**

 **30.6%** THE PERCENTAGE OF MEN WHO HAVE SUFFERED FROM A PERIOD OF DEPRESSION IN THEIR LIFETIME  **4X** (more likely to commit suicide than women)

11% THE PERCENTAGE OF ADOLESCENTS WHO HAVE A DEPRESSIVE DISORDER BY THE AGE OF **18**

16 MILLION

THE ESTIMATED NUMBER OF US ADULTS WHO HAD AT LEAST ONE MAJOR DEPRESSIVE EPISODE IN **2012.**

350 MILLION

THE NUMBER OF PEOPLE GLOBALLY AFFECTED BY SOME FORM OF DEPRESSION.

1 OUT OF **10**

PEOPLE SUFFER FROM MAJOR DEPRESSION AND ALMOST **1** OUT OF **5** HAS SUFFERED FROM THIS DISORDER DURING HIS (OR HER) LIFETIME.

+ + By 2020, depression will be the second leading cause of world disability, and by 2030 it is expected to be the largest contributor to disease burden * +

While many people struggle through depression worldwide, their experiences vary. In the exercise section of this chapter, it's important for you to personalize what depression feels like. Although the sensation can take on many forms, it's important for you to select how it affects you personally to better understand it. By completing this initial exercise, you will have the tools and vocabulary to talk about your depression for future exercises. We also think you'll be surprised that so many people could explain key aspects of what you may be feeling. There's nothing quite like mutual experience to feel understood.

So let's get to work.

EXERCISE

 Draw a picture of yourself when you're depressed or draw a picture of how you envision depression.

Now select as many of the following words and phrases that describe the way depression feels. Feel free to add your own.

DEPRESSION FEELS LIKE/MAKES ME FEEL—

- [ ] **Numbness**
- [ ] **Emptiness/hollow**
- [ ] **Tired (including naps)**
- [ ] **Lonely, isolated**
- [ ] **Like a weight is pressing down on me or that I carry around**
- [ ] **Overwhelming**
- [ ] **Worthless**
- [ ] **Like drowning**
- [ ] **Everything I do feels pointless**
- [ ] **Lack of motivation**
- [ ] **Paralyzed**
- [ ] **Like a wet blanket, a thick fog, or dark shadow**
- [ ] **Like a zombie**
- [ ] **Hopeless**
- [ ] **No motivation**
- [ ] **Sadness**
- [ ] **Reclusiveness**
- [ ] **Like being stuck in a hole or pit**
- [ ] **Constantly seeing the negative**
- [ ] _____
- [ ] _____

"HOUSTON,
WE HAVE A PROBLEM"

(AND YOU KNOW WHAT
IT IS)

CHAPTER 2

If you ask anyone born before 1994 where they were when the September 11, 2001, terrorist attacks occurred, they can tell you what they were doing and what happened afterward.

I was in college and woke up to a phone call from my mom frantically telling me to turn on the TV. My roommate was asleep and told me to turn down the TV, but within seconds I watched in horror as a plane slammed into one of the World Trade Center towers and exploded. I ran down the hallways screaming for everyone to wake up and watch TV.

That day changed my life forever.

By September 25, I was on a plane to Ft. Bragg, North Carolina, to attend Special Warfare Indoctrination and Training. I would then head to the Defense Language Institute in Monterrey, California, to learn another language. By the summer of 2003 I found myself on a small forward operating base in the mountains of Afghanistan right next to the Pakistani border. I would end up enduring sixty-seven different attacks by rockets, landmines, and firefights and live to tell about them.

But I didn't make it out unscathed.

On December 10, 2003, our base came under heavy attack from Taliban and al Qaeda operatives. I was sitting inside a makeshift building with a tin roof and reading Stephen King's The Stand, when the glass in my window exploded and knocked me sideways off my cot. Then the screaming began.

"Incoming! Incoming! Incoming! Get your shit on and let's go!" a fellow solider screamed down the hallway.

I fumbled with my body armor and grabbed my M16 while sprinting out the door. Once I collided with the flimsy wooden door, I shielded my eyes from the sun and sucked in cold mountain air. In my haste, I had no time to put on pants or a jacket, so I continued to sprint toward a bunker in shorts and an undershirt. Another rocket came slamming into the base, and I heard someone yell, "The bastards are targeting the defensive positions!" That statement would end up prophetic.

I continued to sprint until I spotted a red sticky mess in the dust nearby while someone muttered over and over, "You're gonna be okay. You're gonna be okay." Peering around a corner I watched as a medic helped a young Afghan boy no more than fifteen years old. The boy worked with his father on base as a contractor. He'd taken shrapnel to the chest and his lung collapsed. The medic was preparing to jam a large bore needle into his chest to relieve the tension in the lungs. I continued to run, but even though it's been over a decade since that day, I can still vividly recall the boy's face and wide eyes.

To minimize further civilian casualties, a fellow friend and intel solider named Steve and I gathered the locals on base and got them inside a reinforced area near the base's kitchen.

We were the last two inside. *Only we didn't make it.*

When I awoke, a large Afghan man stood over me. His eyes were wild, and he pointed furiously behind me to where Steve would have been. But Steve was nowhere to be found. The blast had thrown him through a door, smashing through the tables and chairs where the soldiers on base would eat. The impact from the blast threw me into a wall that crumpled me like a rag doll and broke my wrist. I also had a severe concussion despite wearing a helmet.

Dazed, I stood and wiped fragments of glass and shrapnel from my forearms while my palms bled in response to the sharp pieces. Stumbling through the door I called out for Steve over the ringing in my ears while the world around me continued to explode.

I found Steve in a corner where he sat sheet white, rocking back and forth, and holding his arm. A trail of blood smeared the floor leading to where he'd crawled. Gently, I reached out and touched him while he continued to rock back and forth.

"Let me see."

Steve continued to rock and said something I couldn't understand due to the underwater sensation I felt in my head and ears.

"Let me see," I told him again while reaching for my knife.

Steve reluctantly let go of his arm. I cut away his blood-soaked sleeve and looked for the wound. At the base of his triceps, loose muscle tissue hung while a large hole poured blood. It almost looked like a pop can had exploded in his upper-arm muscles.

"I gotta move you or we're gonna get blown up again," I told him. Steve nodded, and I stuck my head under the armpit of his good arm while we struggled to stand. Both of us limped along while another solider rushed into the room to help carry my wounded friend.

We could only move a short distance before I leaned him against a wall and patched him up while my heart pounded and fingers trembled. Steve was slipping into shock and needed medical help.

"Stay with him and keep patching him up," I told the other solider. Then I ran out the back door. As I rounded the corner, I ran into a brick wall where, just a few days earlier, they walled off a section of the base that led to triage. I cursed and ran back as fast as I could, but not before another rocket sent me sprawling to the ground, shaken.

When I returned to where I left my wounded friend, I yelled at the other solider, "THEY BLOCKED ACCESS TO TRIAGE! WHERE THE HELL DO WE GO?"

The other soldier had me take over patching up Steve and ran out the entrance where the explosion had occurred. I'd been reluctant and afraid to use that exit. Several minutes later he returned with two shaky medics who took over. I helped as best I could prepping Steve for an IV. One medic's hand shook so badly the other had to take over when they went to stick him with the needle.

Overhead, we heard a jet thunder past and drop explosives on our attackers. Not long after, the assault on our base ceased, and I helped carry Steve to a helipad where an Apache helicopter waited to rush him to a medical center.

I stood on the helipad as the chopper took off while airborne rocks and dirt stung my face until Steve was only a speck on the horizon. Later that evening, after speaking gibberish and incomplete sentences as I assessed my wounds, medics would discover a broken wrist, superficial shrapnel embedded in my lower back, and the onset of a severe concussion (later to become known as Traumatic Brain Injury). I, too, was evacuated to a medical outpost at Kandahar Airfield where I would spend the last month of my tour of duty doped up on pain medication, sporting a fresh cast on my arm, and manning a radio inside the base headquarters.

A week before returning to the United States, a team of replacements from my Army unit arrived. Among them was one of my best friends, Kyle Seitsinger. We had met a few years earlier, and he became close with my family. My mom viewed him as her "third son," and Kyle had his own key to our home. He even visited when I wasn't around. I was ecstatic to see my friend, but also warned him of the dangers he was about to face. His final question before I hopped on a plane back home is the one that still haunts me.

"How did you survive all this and not go crazy from fear?"

The words I left him with always feel empty when I remember them. I wish I would have hugged him instead and said, "Don't worry about that, bro. You'll get through this just like I did."

But my final words to Kyle, my friend and one of the people taking my place in a war-torn country, were these: "The minute you stepped into this country, you were dead. Every day you wake up is another day to die. I had to convince myself I was a dead man walking...and now you are too. If you worry about dying, you'll never do your job. Just remind yourself you're dead already, and maybe tomorrow you'll still be alive."

Kyle was killed on January 29, 2004, two days after I returned home to the United States. I blamed myself. I blamed God. I blamed the war, the military, my friends, and my family. Then I spiraled into a deep and dark depression that lasted well over a year. I no longer knew how to handle what I'd been through or what'd I'd seen overseas. My relationships fractured, and I was struggling with purpose and even the age-old question, "What's the meaning of life?"

PEELING BACK THE ONI0N

If you've ever sliced an onion, you noticed it has several layers before you reach the core. Dealing with your depression and finding the root causes is a lot like peeling an onion. There's a top layer you believe is the cause, but upon further excavation, you find several other layers and a root.

After reading my story where I sank into depression, it's easy for you to say, "Well, of course, you were depressed. You were dealing with loss, pain, and trauma from your past." True, but I was also struggling with existential questions such as purpose and meaning as a cause of the trauma. I also no longer had the skills necessary to deal with stress and the difficult life events I faced.

Here's what's ironic. When I first went to counseling and my counselor asked why I was depressed, can you guess what my response was?

"I don't know."

That may seem like a silly cop-out of an answer, but you know my story and I've spent the time detailing it for you. It's like stepping back from a stained-glass window. Up close it looks like jagged shards, but the farther back you step away, you start to see the whole picture more clearly. Your depression may seem like a series of disconnected and jagged shards. Maybe you've even told yourself or a friend you don't know why you're depressed.

Let's take a step back for a second and see if we can piece those shards together to get a more accurate picture.

 Write out the ten worst moments of your life.

Write ten moments you've been stressed out recently.

Write ten activities your depression keeps you from doing.

We'll explore these answers more fully in the next exercise section and refer to them, so keep this page bookmarked. You'll notice that key pages each have a bookmark icon at the beginning of the exercises for easy reference.

SURVEY SAYS...

In the years I've spent coaching men and women at HeartSupport, I had a hunch that most everyone knows at least a few reasons behind their depression. But mining those results is work. Sometimes the root of our depression may be painful to admit, or other times it can be explained by people or causes close to our hearts.

So I put my hunch to the test. In our survey of 500 men and women, we included a section that asked about reasons behind their depression. We allowed respondents to choose as many answers relevant to their situation. We asked questions such as, "Does past pain or trauma play a part in your depression?" "Are emotional or relational issues part of your depression?"

The results were staggering and revealing. Here's what people told us:

» 369 respondents (75% of those surveyed) told us stress and not knowing how to handle difficult life events was a major reason behind their depression.

» 295 respondents (60% of those surveyed) said emotional issues or relational issues with friends or family played a large part.

» 272 respondents (more than half) claimed past pain or traumatic events were an underlying reason behind their depression.

» 252 respondents (half of those surveyed) informed us they were facing existential dilemmas like finding purpose or a lack of direction in their life that exacerbated their depression.

Other reasons respondents mentioned were these:

» 232 respondents said psychological issues (such as negative thoughts, poor self-image, or mental well-being) were a factor in their depression.

» 192 respondents told us that a physical/medical issue or chemical imbalance were behind their depression.

» 166 respondents said poor choices and moral failings added to their depression.

» 127 respondents let us know spiritual implications (or a lack thereof) were behind their depression.

And here's where the proof is in the pudding as the saying goes. Only sixty-six people chose "I don't know" as a reason behind their depression. However, that information is misleading as all but three people chose other reasons listed as a cause of their depression besides claiming they "didn't know."

We also allowed people to choose "Other" and list a reason, but most of them focused on either self-hate or fell in the relational category because of conflict with family members.

So the survey says, whether you want to believe it or not, there's a good chance you know the reason behind your depression.

Now let's peel back that onion.

EXERCISE

Here are the same choices we gave the people who took our survey. Choose as many as are applicable.

WHAT DO YOU FEEL IS THE REASON BEHIND YOUR DEPRESSION?

- [ ] Stress/life events
- [ ] Emotional/relationships
- [ ] Past pain/trauma
- [ ] Lack of purpose/direction
- [ ] Physical
- [ ] Medical/chemical
- [ ] Psychological
- [ ] Moral/I screwed up
- [ ] Spiritual
- [ ] I don't know*
- [ ] Other_____

*Note: If you find that you truly don't know, that's okay! You may do the work necessary, but it still may seem as if no answers are coming. We encourage you to seek a therapist who can help walk you through this more and determine medical or professional assessment if necessary. There's no shame in going to counseling or a therapist. You're talking about the guy who just told you he spent a year in counseling for depression.

CONNECTING THE DOTS

Look back at what you chose for a reason behind your depression. Were any of your choices the same majority answers other people chose (such as stress/life events, emotional/relational)? It shouldn't come as a surprise if they did, but you're probably wondering why so many people chose the same answers, right?

Since the Industrial Revolution, human life has adapted dramatically. Families once lived in tightly knit communities and children often took on the family trade before the Revolution. However, once the textile and machine industry boomed, many people found their lives different. While we may not want to admit this, to some degree we have become like robots who complete the same tasks every day. While completing mundane tasks is paramount to growth most often (you'll learn more about that in chapters focusing on acedia), it's the perpetual grind and addition of social media plus comfort that's become a catalyst for depression.

Consider this. Most people wake up at the same time, eat breakfast, get in the car, go to school/work, have lunch, leave school/work, get back in the car, go home, eat dinner, watch TV, browse social media, then go to sleep. Along the way, we see our friends posting the highlights of their lives which—by comparison—make us feel as if we're stuck in the grind while they're having the time of their life. We're also perpetually lonely. Pause for a moment the next time you're at a restaurant and watch how many people's heads are buried in their phones as opposed to talking to one another. The face-to-face connection we're hardwired for doesn't happen because we're all so busy seeing what our digital "friends" are up to and then become depressed when our lives don't look as stunning.

When you feel your life is boring by comparison, it's easy to struggle with purpose and get depressed. When all your connections are digital and not flesh and bone, you can become lonely. With so much digital communication and online vitriol toward one another, we struggle to face adversity and what life throws at us. Relationships become fractured, and with the ones we have we don't want to rock the boat, so we stay silent even when conflict may be necessary to move the friendship or romantic relationship forward.

That may sound like an educated guess as to why the reasons behind depression are highest for stress, life, relationships, and pain, but a study reported in the Johns Hopkins Health Review (2017) confirms this with the growing number of teenagers reporting major depressive episodes.

> *Research shows that relational aggression—just the sort that kids inflict on each other via social media—can be more damaging to young psyches than a punch to the gut....Once teens leave home for college, they are thrust into an adult-like world that can be fraught with new challenges and result in added stressors...Visits to counseling centers at universities and colleges increased by 30 percent between 2009 and 2014, according to a recent report from the Center for Collegiate Mental Health at Penn State University.*

This is why it's paramount to "connect the dots" so you can understand your depression and grow stronger by doing so. In the previous section, you may have marked down emotional pain as well as struggling with direction and purpose. One of those deals with your emotional well-being while the other is existential or can be a philosophical issue (which is to say, dealing with purpose and meaning within the realm of your existence and why you're on this planet).

Sometimes your reasons may overlap and other times they may have nothing to do with one another. In this section, we'll use guided steps to draw connections among the reasons behind your depression. If they aren't related, then don't connect them. Instead examine how the events you wrote about in the previous section are affecting your well-being now.

Look back at the reasons you chose behind your depression AND your top ten worst moments (pg. 27 and 32). What patterns do you notice in these situations?

Because of them, what are some things you now believe about life?

What about yourself?

How about others?

Now look back at the top ten stressors in your life and answer the following:

⊘ If you could perfectly control these circumstances, what would you make happen?

⊘ What are you afraid will happen because you can't control those circumstances?

⊘ What patterns do you notice in the situations that stress you out? Are there similar patterns behind your reasons for depression and the things that stress you out? If so, what's the connection?

Finally, look back on the top ten activities depression keeps you from doing and answer the following:

🪐 What is it you believe that keeps you from doing those things?

🪐 What are you afraid will happen if you actually do them?

🪐 How do you connect with others? Do your reasons behind depression hinder those relationships? If so, why?

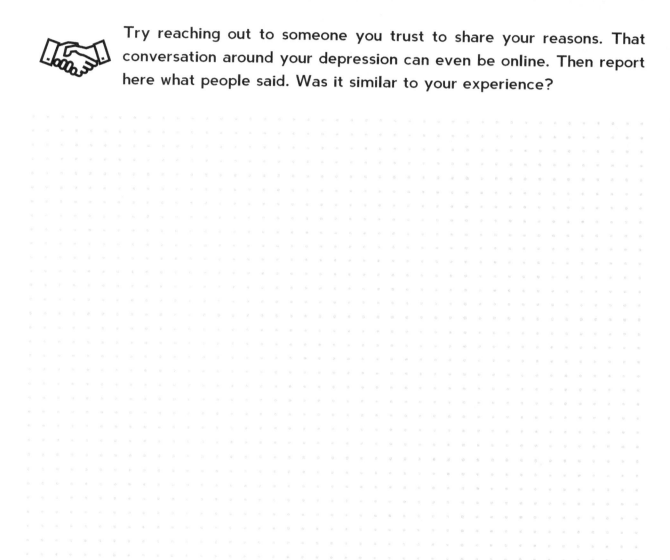

Try reaching out to someone you trust to share your reasons. That conversation around your depression can even be online. Then report here what people said. Was it similar to your experience?

Note: If you don't know a safe online community, we encourage you to head to our Support Wall at heartsupport.com/community.

CONSTRUCTING A
WHOLE PERSON

(AND NOT A
BLACK HOLE)

CHAPTER 3

In January 2018, my wife and I took the month of January to go through the Whole30 program. Whole30 began after the founder, Melissa Hartwig, went to rehab for drug addiction. After rehab, she quit smoking, gave up sugar, and began exercising to reinforce her "growth mind-set"—that she was a healthy person with healthy habits. She opened a CrossFit gym and became a sports nutrition therapist and, in 2009, co-created the Whole30 program. Her thirty-day health- and habit-focused approach emphasizes whole foods and works as a reset for many people to catapult them into healthier lifestyles.

So for thirty days my wife and I had to eliminate sugar, alcohol, grains, beans, soy, and dairy from our diet.

As someone who spends five days a week in the gym and eats healthy, the transition wasn't too difficult, and I welcomed the challenge. But I made a terrible, terrible mistake in thinking I could return to old eating habits and fried foods after completing the thirty days.

Because I'd eaten predominantly bland and healthy foods for thirty days, my stomach became accustomed to that type of food. Instead of following the advice many people suggested and reintroducing foods slowly, I went to the extreme.

The day after the diet ended, I went out with a group of friends to take part in a hot wing challenge where I gobbled down greasy habanero-tossed wings. That evening I woke up with my stomach in knots and running to and from the bathroom.

You'd think I learned my lesson, but I kept eating junk food the next few days and the following week. Soon after, I had stomach cramps, and any time I touched my stomach above my naval a sharp pain shot through my abdomen. I panicked and began googling the symptoms I was having and became convinced I was dealing with stomach cancer or my appendix ruptured (thanks, WebMD).

The doctor convinced me I had developed an ulcer. Because I went crazy after eating so clean, I might have irritated my stomach lining and caused some serious damage. The anxiety of thinking I had cancer also exacerbated the issue and made the pain worse too. But it wasn't an ulcer. After two months of intense stomach pain to the point where I felt nauseated each time I ate, I ended up across the desk from a gastroenterologist. The worst part? All my tests and scans came back clean.

After I completed a heavy round of antibiotics, my stomach pain cleared, and I returned to normal. The doctors correctly diagnosed me with a stomach bug/parasite they think I got from those greasy wings I ate after Whole30.

Before I ever saw a doctor, I had spoken with my family and friends in the medical industry and shared my fears about cancer or other irrational beliefs I had regarding my stomach pain. They assured me I was fine and should see a doctor, but I have to wonder what would have happened if people agreed with my fears. Or imagine if the doctor didn't probe into my eating habits, pain, or my background. Let's say I told him, "I have stomach pain," and his response was, "It's cancer. Let's get you on chemo." He could have easily misdiagnosed me and wreaked havoc on my life.

I share this story because when dealing with depression, instead of asking the right questions of a person struggling through depression, we throw answers that can misdiagnose a person or make the symptoms worse.

In effect, we miss helping the "whole" person and create a black "hole" in someone instead.

THE WHØLE PERSØN

Human beings are complex creatures. Imagine I told you that physical pain is the only thing that's real and everything else is imaginary. If you've ever been through a rough breakup, you'll be the first to disagree with that statement as the emotional pain can hurt just as much as physical pain. You may have even marked emotional or relational pain/issues in the last section and therefore now know just how big a part it's playing in your depression.

In life, a myriad of issues and events can affect you. For instance, if I saw you grimacing and asked, "What's wrong?" you might give me several answers for your pain. You could have gone through a breakup or even broken your ankle. We face moral dilemmas in life. Emotional pain or trauma from the past. Even physical pain. Sometimes we struggle with purpose and meaning. Other times, loneliness and isolation can play into our cravings for community and living connected. These all play a part in the human experience. But when you negate aspects of someone's experiences in life and boil it down to a physical problem when it may be an emotional one, you miss the whole person. Even negating someone's spiritual journey because you find that silly can make their situation worse.

Depression may have several root causes. Let's say you got caught cheating on your girlfriend or boyfriend and you tell me, "I'm depressed," and my response is, "You should take pills. They helped my depression." That's a complete and utter misdiagnosis, isn't it? Sometimes what certain people *don't* need when they're depressed is a pep talk from a friend, but sometimes it is.

History will confirm this. If you'll recall from the beginning of this book, people have searched for a single answer to diagnose and cure depression. For those in history who said prayers or conducted exorcisms or bloodletting, they reduced depression to a spiritual problem. For those who advocated lifestyle changes, working out, or even drugs in our historical records, they saw depression as a chemical imbalance to mitigate through these practices alone. Or consider that by addressing pain and trauma or going to counseling can often navigate only our emotions and feelings.

Isn't it interesting that history has yet to find a real solution for depression that helps everyone? In each circumstance, some people found healing from the various techniques, yet depression has persisted. It can be argued that today the incidence of depression has gotten worse. We've seen a 450 percent increase in depression since 1987 alone.

So we can play this game of, "If not this, then it has to be something else!" We don't integrate the approaches and treat the whole person, because if one approach doesn't work, we discard it.

I would hate for you to reach the end of this workbook and conclude that the team at HeartSupport is trying to create a new fad to combat depression or dismiss past practices that have brought about healing to numerous people across the planet. Instead, we must recognize that just as depression seems to influence our whole lives, it will take a (w)holistic approach to resolve it.

As a human being, you are more than just your physical being or your emotional or spiritual self. You are all of those things and more. Because depression influences all of them, we can learn from history and realize it's not just one problem or one solution, but pieces of each problem, and pieces of each solution. It's an integrated, whole-person approach, which is the end goal as you'll discover toward the end of this book. This is also a good time to state that seeking a therapist or counselor to work through a whole-person approach can be beneficial. Almost the entire staff at our organization has gone through counseling for one reason or another.

Moving forward, you'll notice many of the exercises asking questions that may or may not connect with what you're going through, but were we not to ask them, we could miss the "whole" person and create a "hole" instead. If you're a friend or family member reading this in regard to someone you suspect has depression, it will be essential for you to realize the importance of treating and loving all aspects of your loved one and not just the parts you think need fixing.

Now, let's look into the whole of who you are. Not just the parts.

In what ways do you notice that your depression influences you?

PHYSICALLY

🪐 Your physical body and your relationship with your body

🪐 Your eating habits

🪐 Your sleeping habits

SPIRITUALLY

- Your connection to a higher power

- Your hopefulness or optimism

- Your ability to receive love

PHILOSOPHICALLY/EXISTENTIALLY

- Your experience of your life's purpose

- Your belief that your life matters

INTELLECTUALLY

- Your ability to focus

- Your desire to learn

EMOTIONALLY

- Your self-worth
- Your general disposition
- Your enjoyment of life
- Your ability to regulate your emotions
- Your willingness to try new things

RELATIONALLY AND SEXUALLY

- Your desire to connect with others
- Your romantic relationships
- Your current friendships
- Your experience of pleasure
- Your relationship with your family
- Your self-confidence

THE DWARF
PLANET'S MOON

CHAPTER 4

Early one morning I met at a coffee shop with a friend of mine who asked if we could talk through some struggles he was facing. A few years earlier he went through a dark time when a drunk driver hit his motorcycle and he lost a leg. Not long after, his wife of two months filed for an annulment. We've often talked through his depression and lifelong struggle with it, but this time things were different.

Sipping his Americano, he informed me his depression seemed worse than ever even though he recovered from the loss of his leg and was in a healthy spot with his new girlfriend.

"Tell me what's going on. I need to know details," I asked.

"Well, my day begins early enough and I'm ready to tackle the things I need to. I have a break between clients most days, so I tell myself I'll use the time to accomplish what I need to get done for work, my relationships, and life in general. Chores, bills, you know," he told me.

"Anyway, I do none of it. I'll sleep, or I'll put on Netflix and zone out. Then I run late for appointments and I'm pissed at myself for not doing what I need to. At night it's the same story—more Netflix and apathy. Then I begin to feel indifferent and hate myself that I feel so numb to my circumstances. From there, I spiral. It gets harder to get out of bed every day. I don't go to the gym. I don't practice my spiritual disciplines. I hate myself for it, but I also have little zest for life and I grow increasingly depressed, isolating myself from others and believing this is how it will be forever. I have no idea how to break out of it, and my pills don't seem to help."

Whistling low through my teeth, I then smiled. "Well the good news is it's not quite depression."

My friend stared at me in disbelief having spent most of his life battling the demon of depression. But I held up my hand before he could object: "You're dealing with depression's twin cousin. It's called acedia."

"Ah-seed-e-what?"

ACEDIA AND ME

Acedia (pronounced *ah-SEED-e-uh*) is an old term coined by monks who lived in the desert during the fourth century. Before the Seven Deadly Sins became known to the world, the early Desert Fathers had a list of "Eight Bad Thoughts." One of the most severe thoughts was that of acedia, which the church eventually rolled up under the sin of "sloth" when the seven sins became commonplace.

One would think "lust" would be the one they hammered on given today's religious environment, but it was considered one of the most minor "bad thoughts." The monks viewed lust as a lower form of greed in that you desired something you didn't have. Acedia was one of the most severe and deadly thoughts because of the despair and absolute disdain for life it produced in a human being. It's a shame the word has been lost to ancient textbooks and is no longer used, because acedia's connotations carry far more weight in today's cultural environment.

I first learned the term when I read author Kathleen Norris's book, *Acedia & me: A Marriage, Monks, and a Writer's Life*. In the book she explains: "The demon of acedia—also called the noonday demon—is the one that causes the most serious trouble of all…He makes it seem that the sun barely moves, if at all, and…he instills in the heart of the monk a hatred for the place, a hatred for his very life itself."

Many of the desert monks found themselves in the same place as my friend. Work in the morning, but by noon, they despised the repetitive nature of chores or work. After some time in this condition, they felt little zeal for life. Prayer stopped, sleeping increased, and they felt numb. Eventually, they despised life itself as they spiraled into a dark hole.

This condition can even begin due to traumatic events in one's life. Norris—no stranger to suffering and pain—tragically lost her husband, but instead of spiraling into depression, she found herself battling acedia. She says this:

> *There were so many days when I woke up indifferent to everything, especially when my husband died... When he was alive, the caregiving had to be done so I couldn't be indifferent. But I think one of the worst phases—and I don't want to malign the show because it was kind of entertaining—was when I watched an entire season of America's Next Top Model. In one sitting.*

Reading through the book, I found myself nodding along and remembering times when I thought I'd been depressed only to discover I'd been battling its twin cousin. The good news and bad news, however, is acedia is a condition you can fight, but fighting it can also be mundane and feel as if you're getting nowhere.

It's important to note you can deal with both depression and acedia at the same time. Here's where our dwarf planet analogy gets interesting too. Charon is the largest of Pluto's five moons. Scientists discovered that Charon is gravitationally locked with Pluto and also massive enough that Pluto-Charon is sometimes considered a double dwarf planet. Just as depression and acedia are unique but similar, they both have a part to play and operate in similar functions that can pull on your gravitational well-being.

However, you may be tempted to think, "Oh no! One more thing to add to my list of things that are wrong with me!" Instead, realize this is another aspect of depression that functions differently and is an important part to explore in our whole-person approach to healing.

Before we learn how to combat acedia, let's do some exercises to help you process whether this is part of your journey and impacting your life or not.

Give yes or no answers to the following:

Y   N

☐ ☐ I feel little joy or pleasure in the things I normally enjoy.

☐ ☐ Repetitive tasks like chores, work, or even hanging out with friends have become overwhelming.

☐ ☐ I know there are things I should do, but I don't have the energy to do them anymore.

☐ ☐ I hate/dislike myself/feel worthless because I can't seem to accomplish simple tasks I know I should do.

☐ ☐ When at work or doing menial tasks, it feels like the day is 10,000 hours long.

☐ ☐ I find myself coping or numbing out with things like incessant social media/ Netflix/naps/sleeping/video games.

☐ ☐ I used to feel close to my friends, but now I notice I'm putting distance in our relationship and isolating more.

☐ ☐ I find spiritual practices like prayer/meditation a waste of time or boring now.

☐ ☐ I feel apathetic and indifferent in many areas of my life.

☐ ☐ I lack purpose and direction in my life; whereas, I once felt I knew where I was going.

WHAT THE RESULTS MEAN

If you marked over three to four answers as yes, there's a good chance acedia has snuck into your life. If you marked yes to most, then you are struggling to some degree with acedia. But don't fret. If this is you, we'll show you how to combat the "noonday demon."

THE SPIRITUAL IMPLICATIONS OF ACEDIA

In the previous chapter, we spoke of how important it is not to miss the whole person. When you *only* treat certain aspects of the whole (such as physical, emotional, psychological, spiritual), you can simplify a complex issue. While acedia is a term coined by Christian monks, its aspects are well known to Zen Buddhists who also call it acedia or sometimes "mara." Even famed humanist Aldous Huxley wrote about his struggles with acedia.

If you're shaking your head saying, "Well, I'm not into anything spiritual. It's silly," consider for a moment that according to Pew research, around the world over eight in ten people identify with a religious group. Almost nine out of ten people believe in a higher power with 68 percent of religiously unaffiliated US adults believing in a supreme being. That is a large percentage of the world to ignore such an important aspect of their emotional well-being. Plus, it would be intellectual snobbery to look down our noses at others who are struggling through spiritual ramifications affecting their day-to-day lives.

That being said and laying my cards on the table, when I came home from war to my battle with depression and acedia, I found healing through the Christian faith and became a follower of Jesus. While I was raised in a Christian household and would have culturally identified as a Christian, I found that most within the faith I met were very judgmental and hypocritical. Their spirituality was just a guise for being a "good person." So at age seventeen, I silently left the church, having never believed in faith or spirituality and viewing it as a coping mechanism for weak minds. However, when faced with my own mortality and the question, "What is the meaning of life?" I found that while I loved science, it provided me with a weak answer and only added to my depression.

Within the scientific community the common answer boils down to this: "Life doesn't have a purpose. Get over it. Live free." While an oversimplification, you can google "Does Life Have a Purpose?" and the top scientific articles (along with psychological ones) point to the common assertion we are products of our biological conditioning. Love is a chemical reaction in the brain to advance the species and keep us from annihilation.

Even those who entertained the notion of a higher power for the sake of argument point to there being no real purpose even from a divine creator's standpoint. It would be nothing more than a cosmic experiment. Purpose, therefore, is what you make of it since the species will one day end, which is a pretty bleak way to look at life. Like most people, I wanted to believe love mattered as do human emotions and that I'm on earth for a reason.

Faith, spirituality, and the divine played the biggest part in combating depression for me—and has for many others. Unfortunately, most times it can also be used to bludgeon men and women struggling through depression. What's sad about that style of thinking is that even these early monks and famed preachers such as Charles Spurgeon battled depression so severe, they often found it difficult to get out of bed. Many in the faith traditions of today think depression is a lack of "faith." Yet what's odd is that we have this old term coined by monks who probably had more faith than many in the pews, temples, and mosques today.

This matters because people who shrug and say spiritual matters, purpose, or meaning bears no real thought or importance haven't thought deeply about their life or others. They don't realize you can struggle through existential depression. While we claim to be more enlightened than our predecessors, we're just more entertained. Social media, binge-watching Netflix, and serial dating through the myriad of romantic matchmaking apps has an anesthetizing effect on the deeper questions we should ask and can lead to bouts of depression and acedia.

How we relate to the world and where we derive purpose are important questions we're desperate for and yet dismiss. The mental health crisis alone can attest that many are wandering aimlessly through their existence. Questions about purpose, meaning, the divine, or the absurdity of life make a huge difference in the way we interact with the world and others, and there's a big reason why.

In his book *After Virtue: A Study in Moral Theory*, Scottish philosopher Alasdair MacIntyre uses an illustration about our need for stories to derive meaning.

Imagine for a moment, you're waiting for a bus and a young man walks up to you and says, "The name of the common wild duck is *Histrionicus histrionicus histrionicus.*" While you may understand the sentence the man uttered, it makes no sense without a greater narrative. Perhaps the man is homeless and mentally ill. Maybe he's just mistaken you for someone he met at the library who asked the Latin name for a wild duck. What if he's just come from a therapist's office where he was encouraged to break his shyness by talking to strangers? Or perhaps he's a spy trying to identify his contact.

The first narrative is sad, the second comical, third engaging, and fourth dramatic. His point in the illustration is to show that without a handle on the story, there's no way to understand the meaning or how to answer the young man.

When we ignore the story of life and our purpose, or ask others to, we do ourselves a disservice. We hand out entertaining Band-Aids through our advancement in technology, and yet hit TV shows like *Westworld* that explore the relationship among consciousness, robots, and humans remind us of the continual nagging in our guts that asks, "What is it to be human? What is the meaning of life? Is there something spiritual to all this?"

We will need stories, nights wrestling with our thoughts, engaging conversations, differing viewpoints, and maybe a little faith to combat the numbing agent so many of us have been drinking in today's culture if we are to engage in the battle against things like depression and acedia.

So before we move forward with techniques and exercises to combat acedia, let's see what's playing a role in it. Don't worry, we'll look at it from a spiritual and logical perspective.

EXERCISE

 Choose which questions are the most applicable to you:

I derive purpose and meaning from—

I numb my emotions when I (binge watch Netflix, serial date people, spend hours on social media, drink alcohol or —)

I can spiral into self-hate/self-loathing when I—

What are some things I'm constantly putting off? Why don't I want to do them?

What are spiritual practices I put off or find absurd? Why?

Do you think faith or a lack thereof is playing into your depression or acedia (if you identify more with acedia)? Why or why not?

If you're comfortable exploring the spiritual implications in your life, what are things you think would help you with your depression/acedia?

Ask yourself this question: "Do I even have a spiritual practice?" If so, what's the answer? If you know others who do, how do they find purpose and meaning in life?

COMBATING ACEDIA

I'm willing to bet you were able to fill out the question, "What things are you constantly putting off and why don't you want to do them?" In our day-to-day lives vain repetition sounds terrible and we hate doing it. For instance, if I told you I needed you to stuff 2,000 envelopes with letters, then handwrite the names and different addresses on them, you'd say it was torture, right? We put off things like prayer though we're certain it will enrich our spiritual life. We put off doing the dishes or laundry even though we know we need clean dishes to eat on and clothes to wear.

While finding romance and a significant other is often on the forefront of many young singles' minds, here's something most people forget about staying together "for better or for worse": it can—at times—feel like going through the motions. That romantic infatuation or ooey gooey feeling you once had, with time, will morph into a love of the will. Funny enough, every marriage that has stood the test of time will confirm "love is a choice and action, not just a feeling."

So here's the good news. Combating acedia has simple steps that can help you act and combat the feelings of indifference, self-hate, apathy, and keep you from spiraling further. The bad news is that it begins by choosing to participate in little things that may seem repetitive, but make a big difference.

When we surveyed our 500 respondents battling through depression, we asked a simple question: "What things have helped you cope and battle your depression?" Here's what their answers revealed—**most of the activities that helped were repetitive tasks that could be done daily or weekly.**

What the desert monks found in their battle with acedia was the same. They found joy after they had completed tasks at work even though sometimes the drudgery seemed insurmountable. By pushing through and praying—even in short bouts—they were glad they did. For everyone in this life, discipline often becomes the defining fire by which things like talent or goals become an actual ability. It is indifference and believing it will always be this way that keeps us stuck.

So what simple things can you do to take action steps? Let's dive in.

EXERCISE

Choose from this list the tasks you can do daily or weekly to help you cope with your depression/acedia:

- [ ] Finding a hobby (if so, list it)
- [ ] Connecting with nature
- [ ] Hanging out with a pet
- [ ] Playing music
- [ ] Cleaning
- [ ] Drawing
- [ ] Serving within the community/city
- [ ] Spending time with friends/family
- [ ] Prayer
- [ ] Recreational activities
- [ ] Hiking
- [ ] Writing stories
- [ ] Writing poetry

- [ ] Yoga
- [ ] Exercise
- [ ] Breathing/meditation
- [ ] Going to church/temple
- [ ] Reading
- [ ] Journaling
- [ ] Making new friends
- [ ] Joining an interest group
- [ ] Joining a recreational sports team
- [ ] Skating
- [ ] Painting
- [ ] Going to therapy
- [ ] Spiritual practices

My plan of action is to:

A FINAL NOTE OF IMPORTANCE:

After completing this chapter you may be tempted to think, "Problem solved. I've been dealing with acedia." While that may be the case for some people, remember that in the previous chapter we alluded to peeling back the layers of an onion. Acedia may be one layer, or it could be the root. We must continue to explore each layer, each new planet, and each new discovery while we navigate the vastness of the human experience with depression. Acedia may have its part to play as well as philosophical and existential questions we explored in this chapter, but we must continue to delve into the unknowns behind our emotions and relationships in further chapters.

So let's probe a little deeper into darkness.

LIFE IS A SHIPWRECK:

DON'T FORGET TO SING
IN THE ESCAPE POD

CHAPTER 5

If you're like most people, you listen to certain styles of music on your good days and different songs or albums on your worst days.

Every summer, HeartSupport attends Vans Warped Tour, a traveling music festival consisting of hard rock, pop-punk, and metal bands. At the festival, we have conversations with thousands of men and women in our pop-up tent ranging from depression to relationship problems. The first question I ask is, "What bands are you here to see?" Once they've rattled off the artists they love, I follow up with another question, "What about their music do you love? Has it helped you at all?"

The responses people give us are telling. One young woman told me if it wasn't for her favorite band's music, she wouldn't be alive. It got her through some of the roughest points of depression and heartache she'd ever been through.

I could relate to the way she felt and her story. Before I left the military and while I was fighting in Iraq, my first wife left me and filed for divorce (I'm now remarried). Upon coming home and leaving the Army, I lived on my best friend's couch while drinking myself to sleep most evenings. In the mornings, I would cry in the shower so no one would hear me. With each month that passed, my friend could tell I was sinking deeper into depression. I was isolating, drinking more, and ran around like a zombie.

One evening, however, I found myself at a metal concert where my favorite bands were playing. Before the headliner came on, a band I never heard of took the stage and blew me away. Their lyrics were deep, content relevant, and their stage presence demanded attention. I went home and bought their album, entitled *Messengers*. One song on the album was about the lead singer's struggle watching his parents divorce.

While my life looked like one of those space shipwrecks you see in the movies where everyone's dead and floating around in the emptiness of space, surprisingly I found myself screaming those lyrics at the top of my lungs at home or in the car. I played the song thousands of times. Somehow, despite the deep hole I was in, I found myself singing.

It didn't fix my problems, but the music carried the words I couldn't figure out how to say amid my pain. Little did I know how instrumental that band and album would become in my life. Years later, I would meet the lead singer and volunteer for the nonprofit he founded to help people just like me who were falling to pieces and didn't seem to have the support or resources they needed. The band's name? August Burns Red. The lead singer? Jake Luhrs. He's the founder of HeartSupport—the same organization that published this workbook.

During that stage of depression and hardship in my life, I couldn't see a way out or how things could get better. Maybe you, too, have been on the dwarf planet of depression for so long you can't see a way out. Sometimes we even believe "things will always be this way." But what if the shipwreck of depression could lead us to the shore of a new planet eventually?

Life is a shipwreck but we must not forget to sing in the lifeboats.
—VOLTAIRE

What are some songs that relate to you when you're depressed?

What are some songs that help you feel empowered?

THE PERKS ØF ADVERSITY

We live in a society that empowers us to be more comfortable and independent than ever. I can order food from my phone and have it delivered to my house. Unlike the citizens in many Third World countries, I don't need to travel to a well to drink water. I turn on a faucet (but let's be honest, I drink the filtered stuff and not the tap, just like you). I can sit on my couch all day and remain entertained by video games and movies. Hell, when I run out of toilet paper, I can have it delivered in an hour using Amazon Now. If I don't feel like talking to my neighbors, I can use my garage door opener and park my car without ever saying a word to them.

While technological advancements make life easier, we continue to see rising cases of anxiety, suicide, and depression. We're connected to a global village via social media, yet reports continue to point out our overwhelming feelings of isolation and depression as we compare our online lives to one another.

It's an interesting paradox isn't it? That as our wealth and comfort increase, we feel more depressed? In fact, this phenomenon is known as the Easterlin paradox. In the 1970s, Richard Easterlin provided research showing that although successive generations are usually more affluent and wealthy than their parents or grandparents, people seemed to be no happier with their lives. As countries got richer, their inhabitants didn't get happier.

In a twist of irony, it turns out that hardships, pain, and even tragedy (which disrupt our comfort) seem to play a role in both making us feel better and helping us combat isolation and depression.

If I were to tell you that after the terrorist attacks on September 11, 2001, the suicide rate, violent crime rate, admission to psychiatric institutions, and murder rate in New York City went down, would you believe me? Because that's exactly what happened. During the Blitz bombings on London during World War II the same events also happened. Admissions to psychiatric wards went down. As comfort decreased, resiliency and posttraumatic growth increased.

More often than not, when people experience events that disrupt their comfort and isolation in a shared communal experience, they end up thriving. This is one reason we push community so hard at HeartSupport. We have support forums and live streams anyone can join and find other people going through the same events—the same feelings of depression, and even similar life stories. Together, we've found that several hundred people have rebounded and grown as a result by combating feelings of worthlessness and depression together.

If you'll let it, your depression can catapult you to healing. But it will require you to learn how to lean into uncomfortable emotions. But before we learn more, let's do an exercise that examines just why we isolate, don't connect, or avoid digging into the feelings behind our depression.

EXERCISE

Which of the following tools do you turn to when life gets hard?

☐ Social media

☐ Netflix/Hulu/TV

☐ Video games

☐ Drinking/drugs

☐ Texting

☐ Food

☐ A relationship

☐ Sex

☐ Isolation

☐ Other_____

What are you looking for when you turn to those things?

What are you trying to avoid experiencing?

Whom do you know who faced adversity that you admire? Do you have a hero? Have they struggled with depression or something similar?

How can you use technology in a more positive way and be more present in life?

List the tech you use and the socials you connect with. How do they make you feel?

Are you willing to change your relationship with it or take back control?

UNLEARNING HELPLESSNESS

Psychologist Martin Seligman and a group of colleagues were interested in understanding depression and its effects when they observed an unexpected phenomenon related to fear and learning in dogs.

Seligman's experiment began when they conditioned dogs to expect a small shock upon hearing a tone. Much like Pavlov's dogs who would salivate every time the dog heard a bell ring because of conditioning, these dogs began to expect a shock when they heard the tone associated with the pain.

But what happened next "shocked" the researchers.

Seligman's team put the conditioned dogs into a small box with two compartments divided by a low fence the dog could see and easily jump over. The researchers assumed once they rang the bell, the dogs—knowing the shock was coming—would jump over the fence to escape getting zapped. Instead, when the tone sounded, the dogs would lie down! They even shocked the dogs and nothing happened. The dogs didn't try to escape, but instead accepted their fate, and lay down. However, when the scientists put normal dogs in and administered the small zap, they immediately jumped over the fence and escaped.

The conditioned dogs learned more than just to associate pain with a noise. The dogs also learned that trying to escape the shocks was futile and accepted a situation of helplessness. Seligman thus termed the phrase "learned helplessness," which was extended to human behavior as a model for explaining certain aspects of depression. According to Seligman, many depressed people learn to become helpless and accept that any attempt for things to get better or get off the dwarf planet will be pointless because they have no control over their environments.

After further studying this phenomenon, Seligman also discovered people's thinking habits factored into whether learned helplessness would occur. So before we move forward let's do an exercise where we see whether we've become conditioned to accept our environments.

If you ever failed a test, think back to that moment. What was your response? What was your initial reaction? Pick **ONE** answer closest to what you felt at the moment (not how you feel about it currently):

☐ 1. I'm not that smart. Of course, this would happen.

☐ 2. I suck at tests and this subject anyway.

☐ 3. I was unlucky. Forgot to wear my favorite socks.

☐ 4. My teacher is prejudiced and grades on an unbalanced curve.

☐ 5. My teacher grades everyone hard.

☐ 6. I wasn't feeling good that day.

☐ 7. The test was harder than expected.

☐ 8. I didn't have time to study.

Let's try another one. You applied for a job and got rejected. You think:

☐ 1. I'm a terrible candidate. Who would want to hire me, anyway?

☐ 2. I lack the skills and experience for the position anyway, who was I kidding?

☐ 3. There was a ton of talent in the waiting room that day. Should have selected a different day for an interview.

☐ 4. The interviews were biased.

☐ 5. The selection process to get hired at this company is rigorous.

☐ 6. I felt a little sick that morning and was probably off my game.

☐ 7. The job wasn't the right fit for me anyway.

☐ 8. I could have spent a little more time polishing my resume.

Okay, last one. You go on a date after weeks of texting back and forth on a dating app. Your date seems disinterested and ghosts you after you send some follow-up texts after the date. You think:

☐ 1. They probably thought I was ugly and wanted to date someone better looking.

☐ 2. I'm uninteresting and boring in person, that's why they ghosted me.

☐ 3. There was someone else who was good-looking sitting at the table behind me. Bad luck.

☐ 4. They weren't into the same things as I am.

☐ 5. Dating these days is tough.

☐ 6. I've had allergies/health issues as of late, so probably wasn't bringing my A-game.

☐ 7. Ghosting just shows they're not responsible enough to enter a mature relationship.

☐ 8. They were rude to act the way they did. Good riddance.

While these are hypothetical scenarios, they're ones we experience in life and depending on how you responded can be revealing. If you chose answers #1 or #2 it reveals a pessimistic outlook of hopelessness that's internalized and seen by the individual as a steady source of things that won't change. Answers #7 and #8 view the events more as anomalies and external in which they have an optimistic view that things *can* change.

Because these are hypothetical situations and not how you feel when it happens, you may have chosen an optimistic outlook, but the proof is what happens when these events happen in real life. If you default to feelings of worthlessness or a negative outlook, then there's a good chance that when given the opportunity to step off the dwarf planet of depression, you may just stay, because you believe there's no way things *could* change.

But it doesn't have to be that way.

If you remember our survey of 500 people, then there's something interesting about the data people provided: 75 percent of respondents said stress and difficult life situations were the number one reason behind their depression. Relational issues with others and not knowing how to handle their emotions also affected 60 percent of those who responded. Unresolved past pain and lacking purpose or direction in life accounted for more than half of all respondents.

These data reveal that men and women struggling through depression lack the training to face adversity or learn how to become resilient in the face of stress and difficult situations. Even dating and relationships with friends and family have become overwhelming. Just like the dogs who got zapped enough, instead of finding a way out, they've learned helplessness and learned to accept that these events can't change and have fallen into the pit of despair.

We can learn how to cultivate optimism instead. But you have to be willing first. Only then can you reach new worlds and, along the way, sing in the lifeboat.

EXERCISE

 Write ten examples of times when you felt helpless. This could be when someone you know committed suicide, you got fired, someone rejected you, you got cheated on, bullied, and so on.

CULTIVATING OPTIMISM AND CHOICE

If you notice in the previous exercise, most of the circumstances you listed have to do with actions other people did that you weren't able to influence or determine, right?

While it's true we can't make decisions for those people, what's also true is that we *can* make decisions for ourselves. Author Stephen Covey explains it this way: "Between stimulus and response lies man's greatest power. His ability to choose." You may feel powerless or have never realized you hold the power of choice, but we all have this ability. In each scenario in life, we have the power to choose how we respond, especially when other people do something that may hurt us or worsen our depression.

Recently, a team member of ours named Nate had someone in his life commit suicide. In particular, it was someone he was trying to help. When Nate got off a phone call one Monday evening, he could tell that his earnest attempts to encourage his friend were of little help. So he called the next day, but the friend didn't pick up. He called again the next day, and when they didn't pick up, worry set in.

Nate decided to text him to force his hand so he'd respond—"Bro, if you don't call back by tonight, I'm calling the police." When his friend didn't respond, he followed through, now worried something was very wrong. When the police arrived, no one opened the door but the porch light was on. The police said everything appeared normal, but later that evening his friend overdosed.

Nate's initial reaction was anger. When I asked him how he was doing, he responded, "All I want to know is why he didn't pick up the f***ing phone." Nate was honest with our team about his emotions. He was so mad at his friend. Mad that he gave up. Mad that he didn't grab Nate's hand when Nate reached out for him. Like many people who've lost someone to suicide, Nate felt a sense of guilt for not having done enough, but in that moment he realized something profound.

He could choose to let anger or guilt swallow him, or he could choose to believe something else. That afternoon Nate took time to write out his thoughts to explore his emotions, and he discovered that his anger was buried under something beautiful. He realized the work he does each day at our organization matters. Real people's lives are at stake. Some people threatening to kill themselves do. Some people walking through depression want to give up just like his friend. But Nate saw that each day was an opportunity to keep some of them from following through. He could have let himself get swallowed, but he chose a different response to a friend's suicide.

I know it's not always as easy as Nate's example to shift your perspective. It may even sound impossible. Most of us don't take the time to even pause and think, "Man, these emotions I'm experiencing could swallow me alive," but it *is* something we can develop. One way that could be helpful for kick-starting a practice of building optimism as opposed to helplessness is to look back at those ten times you felt helpless and to write (1) the choice you made, and (2) a better choice you could have made that would have helped you feel more empowered and less helpless.

So let's begin by doing that and then I want to show you another technique that will make each day "awesome."

Look back at the ten times you felt helpless. Now write:

1. The choice you made when you felt helpless
2. A better choice you could have made that would have helped you feel more empowered and less helpless.

THE JAR ØF AWESØME

In his book, *Tools of Titans: The Tactics, Routines, and Habits of Billionaires, Icons, and World-Class Performers*, famed author Tim Ferriss shares a technique that's helped him cultivate optimism because he normally sees the negative in life. At home, he keeps a mason jar with the glittered words *JAR OF AWESOME* on it. Every time something cool, exciting, or joyful happens in the day, he writes it down and sticks the note in the jar like clockwork.

He explains: "When something great happens, you think you'll remember it three months later, but you won't. The Jar of Awesome creates a record of great things that actually happened, all of which are easy to forget if you're depressed or seeing the world through gray-colored glasses."

That may sound cheesy to you, but it works. If you never appreciate small wins, then when the big ones come along they won't matter either. It also helps remind you that things aren't as bad as they seem, and you'll begin to see you're growing stronger almost daily.

But what if nothing great happens that day or you can't think of anything? Ferriss says: "[Writing down] 'I didn't die today!' is a reliable winner. That's totally awesome compared to the alternative."

I think so too.

CHALLENGE!

Try creating your own Jar of Awesome or creating a daily gratitude list where you write something down each day. You can even write thank-you cards to people who've helped you and empowered you or write in your list, "I'm getting stronger every day," if you can't think of anything.

Here are other tips to cultivate optimism you can check off to remind you to try:

- ⊘ Place Post-It notes on a computer/car dash.

- ⊘ Set an alarm reminder.

- ⊘ Identify and seek someone who you think has been successful in handling a life event you are facing. Ask them for advice and tell them that their story helped you.

- ⊘ Seek positive news on the internet and intentionally absorb positive things.

- ⊘ Change up your social media feeds and seek to follow people who are positive and have a growth mind-set. This can help change your feeds to be more positive.

- ⊘ Listen to personal development podcasts.

- ⊘ Visit our Support Wall, listen to our truth audio clips, or watch our videos on heartsupport.com for inspiration on how to overcome.

WHAT'S HIJACKING YOUR MAINFRAME?

(IT'S NOT ALIENS)

CHAPTER 6

Even if you did each of the exercises you wrote to bring about gratitude, a sense of well-being, and happiness, here's a simple, yet hard truth. **Happiness is not a realistic state of being.** You will spend most of your life *not* being happy. That may sound terrible at first, but it's not a bad thing. In life you'll be excited, anxious, joyful, fearful, frustrated, and hopeful. Sometimes all at once.

Our emotions help us navigate the trenches of life, but they aren't ultimate means to an end nor should they dictate our day-to-day life and reactions. Imagine a teenager comes to you and says, "I feel I would be happier if I murdered the school bully." We know that's an irrational response and emotion to a complicated problem they're facing. The same could be said of those in long-term relationships who pronounce, "I just don't feel in love anymore." Realistically, they were probably in that relationship because of what they got out of it or the way it made them feel as opposed to a long-term commitment that has trials.

When we make our emotions the thing that dictates our direction, responses, or how we constantly feel, we miss out on opportunities to take action steps. If you've seen the Disney movie, *Inside Out*, it will help you understand this concept. In the movie, the main character and emotion, Joy, tries to run the control panel of the mind for a preteen named Riley. She tries to keep happy all the time and mitigate the other emotions, especially Sadness. Toward the end of the film, Joy realizes that the other emotions like Sadness, Anger, and Disgust all have critical roles to play to create a well-rounded Riley. Some of Riley's favorite memories become those of mixed emotions of Joy *and* Sadness.

Just as one planet does not create a solar system, one emotion like sadness does not define our reality. We need all of our basic emotions working in harmony for a whole life so we can create a balanced and healthy experience. Just as multiple planets create the awe and magnificence of the solar system, your emotions combine to create complex and wonderful emotions to be explored.

In your life, you may feel as if depression has hijacked the mainframe of your mind. But as stated, there are other emotions to explore in the solar system that make up your life. However, when you emphasize one over the other or make them the source of where you find meaning, you'll be sorely let down and progress will become stunted. So in this next exercise we'll explore the sources of our emotions and why we feel the way we do when we get depressed.

EXERCISE

RANK YOUR EMOTIONS
with 1 being the most often.

-------- Sadness

-------- Disgust

-------- Fear

-------- Anger

-------- Joy

-------- Surprise

-------- Trust

-------- Anticipation

-------- Impatience

-------- Criticism

-------- Vulnerability

-------- Embarrassment

-------- Boredom

-------- Loneliness

-------- Depressed

In the movie *Inside Out*, the turning point for Joy was realizing that when Riley felt Sadness, it signaled her parents to come and comfort her, turning a moment of sadness into one of her fondest memories because she felt loved and understood.

 In the same way that Joy realized the potential for Sadness to be a tool for good, in what ways can your base emotions be helpful too?

ΞXPANDING YØUR VØCABULARY

What's interesting in the last exercise you completed is that often the perception of our emotions is determined *by the words* we use to describe our feelings.

For instance, I have a tendency to overcommit and become overwhelmed. When my list of obligations for work and people reach a critical mass, I shut down or lash out in anger. While I would use the words *stressed* or *overwhelmed* to describe what I feel to friends or family, what's really underneath that is fear. I'm afraid to fail and I'm afraid to let people down. I'm afraid because I want everyone to like me and think well of me. But that's not a realistic state of being, and as the saying goes "an empty cup cannot fill another." So I overcommit and become overwhelmed because I'm afraid to let others down because I think they'll hate me.

Once I saw that a fear of people's approval was the source of my problems, I could act and put boundaries in place and exercise my "no." That felt way more empowering than just running through life constantly overwhelmed and trying to make everyone happy because, as we said, happiness all the time is an unrealistic state of being.

So let's expand the emotional vocabulary you use around your depression to understand what may be underneath.

What other emotions on the previous list might you be lumping together and calling depression?

What are emotions you might experience before or in the midst of your depressive episodes that might be more helpful to focus on?

For example, instead of loneliness, that feeling could just be an anticipation for connection. It's easier to do something when you're eager for connection than when you're lonely. Loneliness puts you on the defensive wishing someone would care for you, but anticipating connection puts you on the offense to actively seek connection with someone.

OKAY, WILL I EVER BE HAPPY?

Whether you consider yourself a religious person, an atheist, or something in between, there's something interesting to be found in a few of the famous words of Jesus Christ. In one of his most well-known sermons entitled "The Sermon on the Mount," he shares a seemingly counterintuitive response to people going through life's trials. Check out these paradoxical insights:

Blessed are the poor in spirit,
for theirs is the kingdom of heaven.
Blessed are those who mourn,
for they will be comforted.
Blessed are the meek,
for they will inherit the earth.
Blessed are those who hunger and thirst for righteousness,
for they will be filled.
Blessed are the merciful,
for they will be shown mercy.

Notice he doesn't say, "Blessed are the blessed" or even "Blessed are those who gain fame and money, for they will find happiness." It's the exact opposite. Those who show others mercy, get mercy. Those who mourn, get comforted. Those who are meek are recognized by others.

Most of us believe we'd be happy if we won a million dollars, got a new car, or if our depression up and disappeared the next day. But look at how many lottery winners end up broke and miserable. Remember that ten years from now your new car will probably be on its way to a junk heap. And your depression? It may come roaring back if someone you love cheats on you or if you lost your best friend. Happiness can always get snatched away in a heartbeat. So once again, it's just not a realistic state of being all the time.

The question we *should* ask is how we can cultivate a happy spirit in the midst of depression. That is what's profound about "The Sermon on the Mount." Instead of seeking happiness directly, it's often the by-product of something else. That's why it's so elusive during depression because happiness is something we constantly want and try to force into existence.

For example, let's say you decide, "I should try painting because it can help ease my depression by getting my mind off of it and that would make me happy." The chances of it working are low because you're trying to force something you don't feel. However, let's say you love writing and art. During one of your depressive bouts you sit down, write stories, and draw characters for a book you want to write. In this instance, by doing the thing you love, you're more apt to discover joy as a by-product even though you feel depressed.

To discover where we're being misled, let's look at some examples of activities we think we believe will make us happy. After that we'll explore some activities we enjoy doing to discover joy as a by-product to further gratitude and service along our journey and off the dwarf planet.

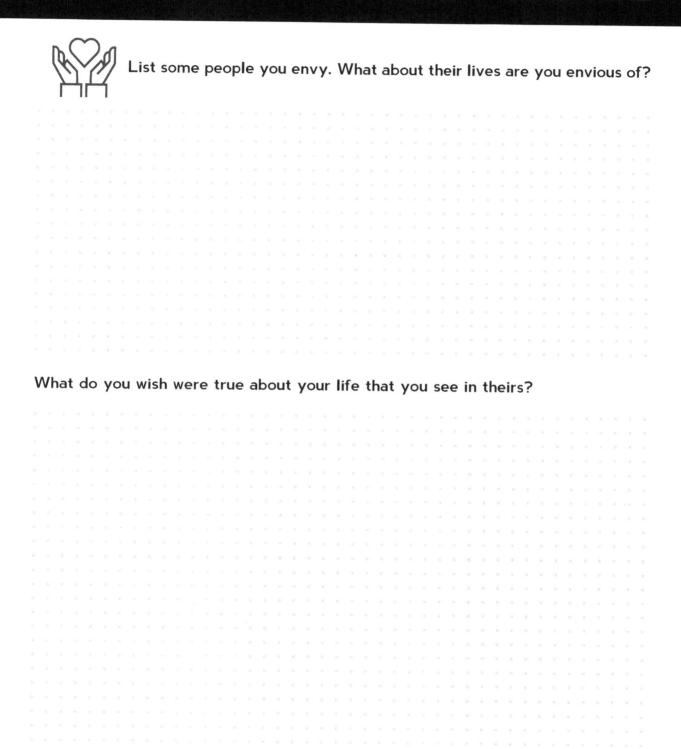

List some people you envy. What about their lives are you envious of?

What do you wish were true about your life that you see in theirs?

List a few things you care about that you've decided you'll never be able to do (*example: I'll never be able to ____, go to ____, be a ____, be with ____, have ____*).

Fill in the blank with as many things as you can think of:

IF I COULD JUST _ _ _ _ _, THEN I'D BE HAPPY.

----------------------------------   ----------------------------------

----------------------------------   ----------------------------------

----------------------------------   ----------------------------------

----------------------------------   ----------------------------------

----------------------------------   ----------------------------------

----------------------------------   ----------------------------------

----------------------------------   ----------------------------------

Now list how you would feel if you got those things, but they were taken away.

I'D FEEL:

----------------------------------   ----------------------------------

----------------------------------   ----------------------------------

----------------------------------   ----------------------------------

----------------------------------   ----------------------------------

----------------------------------   ----------------------------------

----------------------------------   ----------------------------------

----------------------------------   ----------------------------------

Now write down as many things you love doing. A great way to figure this out is to ask yourself, "If I could do anything I loved and not get paid for it, what would I do?"

Now that you have the activities that bring you joy, write out an action plan to implement them into a daily or weekly routine. For instance, I love getting to write articles on medium.com and always having new ideas pop up, so I make it a point every Sunday afternoon to sit down and write for two hours. The by-product is always joy that I am able to do something small I love. For you, it may be something like, "Serve at an animal shelter each Friday." Whatever the case, write out some ideas and then commit to doing them.

MY ACTION PLAN:

A FINAL NOTE:

In our approach to whole-person healing, we recognize that there can be chemical imbalances in some people and don't want to negate the men and women who've fought for healing yet continued to find little joy no matter what they do. At that point it may be time to explore other options and see a professional. Today, in Western medicine, medication has received both praise and stigma, and results can vary. The truth is that for depression diagnosed by a professional, sometimes medication may be recommended. In order to embrace the totality of possibility in your healing and recovery, consider all options, ask questions, and know that it can take a little time and patience to turn the corner.

From personal experience, I was prescribed an antidepressant for over a year while recovering. While the antidepressant worked mildly for me, I found healing through other practices laid out in this book. With each person, experiences differ, and friends of mine have benefited greatly from medication. As with any medication it is important to discuss all medical history and concern with your doctor before starting any new medication.

NAVIGATING RELATIONAL ASTEROID BELTS AND DEPRESSION

CHAPTER 7

*NOTE:

If you're a friend or a family member curious how you can help, this section will be essential.

Late one evening I stumbled out of a dusty building like a drunk pirate not quite used to walking on land. My head was spinning from the news I received. I wanted to vomit and scream all at the same time. The Iraqi base I was stationed at in the middle of Ramadi remained still while the whirl of generators filled the night, my shuffling adding to the noise. Taking another step, I collapsed into the dirt and wept until my tears formed mud on my hands and face.

It would be my friend Greg who would find the shell of a man lying on the ground with a muddy, tear-streaked face.

"She's leaving. She's leaving—god, she's really leaving" is all I managed to get out while sobs racked my body.

Thirty minutes earlier I'd gotten the devastating news about the end of my relationship back home. Iraq was a hard enough place to deal with anyway, but now the person I loved most was gone. Greg leaned me against his barrel-shaped chest and hugged me while I cried. What he said that night made all the difference.

"You're not alone, and we'll get through this together."

Ten years later, I would find out Greg had been diagnosed with cancer a second time. My wife and I crammed my family into the car to spend a week with him while he fought for his life. When we arrived, he met my daughter, and

I played with his two-year-old son. Before I left, I prayed for him and told him the same thing he told me several years ago on a lonely evening in Iraq: "I'm here for you. You know that, right? We'll get through this together."

Greg passed away at 2:20 p.m. on Friday, August 25, 2017, having lost over a hundred pounds as the cancer consumed him. I got the call from one of the team members in our old Army unit, Jake, who'd flown in from New York to spend his last days with him.

Jake and I spoke almost every day after Greg's death retelling stories about him, often laughing and crying at the same time. Both of us had gone through hardships and bouts of depression, and each time Greg had been there for us reminding us we weren't alone.

I didn't take his death well and found myself in that wet blanket of depression mingled with sadness for over a month. This time was similar yet different from what I'd experienced with depression in the past.

Late one night my wife wrapped her arms around me while I cried and mumbled, "I'm just so damn sad. I feel so damn empty. Just…depressed."

Wanna guess what she told me?

THE POWER OF "YOU'RE NOT ALONE"

Telling someone they're not alone in their depression may sound cliché—stupid even. Many would assume "how on earth would a trite sentiment help anyone going through depression?" But they'd be wrong. There is something powerful that happens when people empathize with someone going through a dark time.

When we asked our 500 respondents what the *one thing* someone should tell a friend struggling with depression, over 90 percent of respondents gave us the same answer. What did they tell us? **Letting someone know they're "not alone and I'm here for you" was the best way you could support them.** Sounds crazy, right? But since you're reading this book to understand your depression or make proactive life changes, that's probably what you might have said. Most of the other responses focused on perseverance and reminding a friend not to give up. Others stated reminding a depressed person they're not a burden was powerful.

Here's the hard part, though. Parents, friends, spouses, girlfriends, boyfriends, and employers are not mind readers. We want them to be, but that's not the case. A friend once complained about her core group of girlfriends. She explained that they hadn't reached out to her though she was going through a rough time and that only compounded her depression.

So I asked a simple question: "Have you told them what you need or what you're going through?"

She hadn't. She'd expected them to know and sense it out, even though she told her friends she was "fine." If your friends or family members don't learn what you're going through, you can't expect them to be there for you during your seasons of depression. It should go without saying that the people you confide in have to be safe people. Once you confide in a safe friend or family member, I'll bet you'll be surprised at how many of them can relate to what you're going through. In life, most everyone will walk through a season on the dwarf planet, so the chances of their walking with you and practicing empathy are high.

That may sound scary to open up about how you're feeling, but think for a moment about some of the bravest people you know. I'm willing to bet they're the ones who shared about their lives in authentic ways. Whether that was sharing their fears or past mistakes, when they stepped into a vulnerable space, it seemed courageous. Keeping with our space theme, we like to call these people our "First Mate." They've been through hardship, and by seeking to have at least one person willing to walk through the valley with you—yet not get stuck—is key. So let's take a moment to explore people we could talk to and who could support us in the next exercise.

Three safe people I know are—

1. _____

2. _____

3. _____

If I told them I was struggling with depression, they would respond:

In an ideal world where you're sure they will support you well, what would you tell them? How would you want them to support you?

My greatest fear in telling someone about my depression is—

In an ideal world where they have the means to give you what you need and you're certain you could never burden them, what would you ask from these people?

Imagine you told someone, and they responded poorly. How could you bounce back? What response could you choose that would get you back on your feet and headed in a positive direction?

Who have I supported when they were down and how did that make me feel?

(Note: There is a gift in learning to receive from others and often the exchange of compassion between people is life changing. Let people know what you need and ask others what they need and how you can support them. This can create a depth of connection—real, raw, and genuine that everyone needs and seeks. In fact once you complete all these exercises, it may be helpful to show your First Mate.)

PATCHING YOURSELF UP POORLY

Imagine for a moment I suggested everyone reading through this workbook should take cocaine and do meth to cure their depression. Would you call me irresponsible? Insane maybe? What's interesting is that many of us who've gone through depression will try anything to escape the feelings or the numbness. Many times drugs and alcohol can become those coping mechanisms that spiral us further down the rabbit hole.

Alcohol abuse became how I would cope, and more often than not it left me more depressed. Once again, we surveyed our respondents and asked, "What things have you tried that didn't work in helping your depression?" Here's a list of the most common answers:

- Alcohol
- Drugs
- Ignoring my depression
- Dealing with depression alone
- Self-harm
- Isolating
- Wrong medications/therapists
- Pornography/sex
- Romantic relationships
- Suicide attempts

Many of the respondents told us how much these coping mechanisms made their depression worse. If you'll remember back to my initial story of when I was wounded in action and had to "patch up" my friend Steve, think about what would have happened if we only patched him up? Eventually he would have bled out and died. While destructive coping mechanisms can provide a quick "patch," they are not healing, not restorative, nor transformational. They aim for an immediate change of feeling or distraction, but fail at providing the depth or growth that people truly seek.

None of the things on this list offer genuine connection and can become an excuse for people to not want to try other methods. There is also a deep sense of shame men and women feel resorting to these quick patch techniques. Often they don't want to talk about it. Instead, quick fixes operate like black holes where there's no light and nothing escapes, leaving you to bleed out. Pushing past these old ways and mind-sets of coping is where the healing and balance happen while returning us to orbit.

In any difficult situation in life, we create environments that help us deal with what we're going through, and because depression is no different, there are healthy coping mechanisms and unhealthy ones. You have already completed a list of activities you take joy in doing. Now let's look at what you've tried or know is an unhealthy coping mechanism to make sure you're not sabotaging your relationships or progress.

EXERCISE

What hasn't worked for you? List them.

Thinking back on some things that worsen your depression, let's imagine you're having a pretty positive day, and then you get sideswiped by intense feelings or emotions. In the past, this would most likely have sent you into a downward spiral. You might have felt stuck for days in a hole of depression you didn't feel capable climbing out of. But let's imagine how you could respond to help sidestep that interruption and continue on the positive path your day was on.

Write out your top three to five signposts or actions that exacerbate your depression.

1. ---

2. ---

3. ---

4. ---

5. ---

Now write out how you could respond in a strong and resilient way to those circumstances so you could continue on a positive path.

(Note: This exercise may be difficult to answer, but I want to show you something quickly before you write your responses if you're having a difficult time imagining how you could respond positively. Close your eyes for a second and imagine a beautiful beach. Did you see it? For a brief few seconds you controlled your thoughts. This should be a freeing experience that could apply to our ability to make change and continue on a positive path.)

I CAN RESPOND:

AVOIDING RELATIONAL LANDMINES

Throughout life we've watched tragedies unfold before us in which people have differing opinions. Perhaps the most recent example has been the reactions to police shootings of young African American males. From Ferguson, Missouri's riots over the death of Michael Brown to Eric Garner's death in New York City, we watched our social media feeds erupt into arguments with little compassion over losing a human life. Instead, they became fodder for whatever view people held. The sad part is that the families of the victims, who were mourning, even became targets of people's opinions.

Imagine if you had been the mother, father, sister, brother, or spouse of the slain men and someone told you, "Well, if they had just complied, they wouldn't be dead," or "You should be proud. They died as heroes to the cause." How much rage and anger would you feel? How invalidated in the midst of mourning would those accusations be? Or to drive the point home more, how would you feel if you told your parents or a friend, "I'm struggling with depression," and their response was, "You'll get over it. Just focus on the positive."

I imagine that response would be crushing.

When we asked the men and women we surveyed what the worst possible thing you could say to someone struggling with depression, here were their top answers:

- "Just get over it."
- Some form of guilt trip to make them feel awful about having depression (For example: "I understand, but you need to pull it together for your family. We did when we were struggling.")
- "It gets better. Just focus on the positive."
- "This is just a phase you're going through. It'll pass."
- "Your depression isn't real. You're just faking it for attention."

Comments that invalidate someone's emotions who's come to you in a moment of vulnerability and sincerity—and not met with compassion and empathy—do far more harm than good. Up to this point, perhaps you've wondered how you can ensure you're picking safe relationships to confide in. Maybe you wish you could show a loved one how they could help.

No sweat, we'll show you how to pick a First Mate in this upcoming section.

THE FIRST MATE

In another book the team at HeartSupport wrote covering the topic of self-harm, we explained just how instrumental listening to someone struggling is. The example we shared is that most people can recall the time when they were asked to repeat back word-for-word what their spouse or significant other said. What's amazing is they can typically repeat the basic gist of what their loved one said or perhaps even the full conversation.

But the next words that leave your significant other's mouth are: "You're just not hearing me!"

Stephen Covey, in his book *The 7 Habits of Highly Effective People*, lists habit number five as "Seek first to understand, then to be understood." Listening is something many of us don't do well. More often than not we want to be understood so we can get our point across. A lot of times when someone is talking, we may be already formulating a response in our head, grabbing key parts of the conversation, only to miss the meaning entirely.

When you listen to reply, you end up not fully understanding or empathizing. You can even devalue the discussion by injecting your experience in it when you decide what the other person means before he or she finishes communicating.

Have you ever said the following? "Oh, I know just how you feel. I had the same thing happen," or "Let me tell you what I did in a similar situation."

Covey explains that we often listen "autobiographically" and tend to respond in one of four ways:

Evaluating: You judge and then either agree or disagree.
Probing: You ask questions from your own frame of reference.
Advising: You give counsel, advice, and solutions to problems.
Interpreting: You analyze others' motives and behaviors based on your own experiences.

Covey explains that there may be resistance to hearing these autobiographical messages because, after all, you're just trying to help by drawing on your own experiences to relate. While this technique may be appropriate in some responses—such as from friends or family members who have also struggled with depression—most times instead of seeking to understand another's point of view, you're comparing it to your personal experience, and it negates what they're feeling. Most couples that end up in a counselor's office, for instance, typically mutter these words: "He (she) just doesn't listen to me!"

When going through depression, what most of us desperately desire is for someone to first establish trust with, and that begins when a friend or loved one asserts they're there to listen—and never to judge. If you've ever attended a 12-Step meeting, one essential rule toward recovery and safety is when someone in the group shares, you do not respond with life advice or try to fix their situation. It's a time for them to share their hurts, emotions, and hang-ups.

Think of it this way. In many science fiction films and TV shows, there's a second in command or First Mate. When the Captain is in distress and faced with tough calls and decisions, the First Mate is often there to encourage them to stay the course. If you've ever watched Star Trek or seen the movies, Spock is a great example of someone who doesn't try to fix Captain Kirk, but always believes in him and encourages him to push forward when he falters. A First Mate does the same by listening and encouraging progress as opposed to trying to become the Captain.

Learning to communicate effectively begins by listening. When you find someone to listen and empathize actively, it shows they love you and care about what you have to say and are feeling.

So let's do one final exercise to solidify the people we want to help us along this journey.

EXERCISE

 Look back at the names of the three safe people you wrote down. Which of them are good at listening and would be a First Mate along your journey?

(The reason we suggest having three people is it can become overwhelming to place everything on just one person. This ensures that when one person is unavailable, you have two other advocates.)

MY FIRST MATE[S] IS/ARE:

To avoid potential landmines in your relationships, list the top three things you don't want to hear if you told someone you're struggling with depression:

1. --

2. --

3. --

In order for my friends or loved ones to know what not to say and how to walk with me in our relationship through this, my plan of action is to—

COLONIZING THE SOLAR SYSTEM

(EVEN WHEN YOU'RE AFRAID TO TRY)

CHAPTER 8

Imagine for a moment that humans jump on board with Elon Musk's space programs and colonize the solar system. We start with Mars and send men and women to terraform the planet. They're the first pioneers and, as such, live and die on Mars. It's a one-way trip after all. As technology increases, more men and women are sent to Mars and continue to work in brutal conditions to create a habitable landscape for humans.

You find yourself as a worker in a mine with barely survivable working and living conditions, but as a pioneer, you're proud knowing the legacy you're leaving for mankind.

Only it's not true.

The solar system has been cultivated for the past 700 years. People live out as far as Neptune's moons and humankind is now caste based. You're a slave and will live and die a slave.

One day you learn of an uprising and are offered a chance to infiltrate the highest levels of the infrastructure. But you don't take it. You reason, "We've been slaves this long and someone else surely tried. Better to stay where I am and with what I know than die trying."

WHY BOTHER?

This hypothetical sci-fi situation is actually the premise for one of my favorite trilogies, *Red Rising*. Only the main character actually joins the uprising and thus begins his journey from slave to rebel leader. I won't spoil the ending for you (because I want you to read the series), but the trilogy has a deeply satisfying ending.

Similar to the main character in the *Red Rising* novels, you too may feel as if you're a slave, but just to your depression. Maybe you've even had the thought: "Why bother, it will always be like this. I've tried before." Or maybe you've tried to find a shortcut to healing. But there are no shortcuts, hard as that is to hear.

Unfortunately, we are now a culture built on speed and laziness. How many times have you been upset because the internet on your phone didn't load fast enough only to exclaim what a piece of junk it is? Yet, in the mid-2000s you would have marveled at the ability just to have internet on a phone. Don't want to leave home to get groceries either? There are entire companies like Instacart and Favor that will shop for you and deliver your produce straight to your doorstep. So it makes sense that we want instantaneous results, and if that's what you're expecting of this workbook, then you'll be let down.

Like you, I wanted my depression to end quickly. I wanted to bounce back. Instead, the time I spent after returning home from war and taking proactive steps made subtle but effective changes. One night I shared with a fellow friend and staff member Nate (whom you heard about earlier) on how I felt as if I either had to make instantaneous changes or just give up. What he told me changed my life:

"Ben, there's nothing to fear when you stay stuck or you finally achieve your objective. It's like staying at zero percent or reaching one hundred percent. There's no risk of rejection, failure, or defeat because if you never start, you believe you're safe from those things. But if you're already at a hundred percent, there's no risk because you achieved your goal."

What Nate told me made sense. I wanted instantaneous changes, and any time there were setbacks I believed I'd failed. But no matter how great the oppression or resistance you're facing, freedom is on the other side of the fight. Now that we're approaching the end of this workbook, perhaps there's been progress but maybe there have also been a lot of setbacks. So before we move forward let's discuss our fear and excuses about future progress.

What are some of your best excuses? Lay it all out here.

We're defining an excuse as anything you tell yourself to make it easier mentally or emotionally to accept that you've decided not to do something you know you want to do or would improve your life.

Now let's talk fears.

I'M AFRAID THAT I'LL:
(for example, never get any better). List as many as come to mind.

When you feel these fears? Do you remember why?

What do you do when you feel the fear?

What if you faced your fear and rose above it? Would you feel unstoppable?

THE COURAGEOUS MIDDLE

Consider the story line from the fantasy novel and movie *Harry Potter* for a moment. A young boy discovers he has a magical heritage and attends the Hogwarts School of Witchcraft and Wizardry. With the help of his friends, he faces an attempted comeback by the dark wizard Lord Voldemort, but decides the task is far too dangerous, drops out of the school, and gives up.

If you're shaking your head saying, "That's not how the story goes!" you're correct. But imagine if that's how the story ended? Pretty lame, right? I show you both *Harry Potter* and *Red Rising* to point out just how terrible stories would be if our favorite characters gave up.

In every great story, what makes or breaks the narrative is the space in between doing nothing and achieving victory, and if art imitates life, then that's what makes or breaks our story too. The middle-of-our-story/moments of insurmountable odds is where we see courage flourish. The day Nate challenged me on my mindset of all or nothing he shared about something he calls the "Courageous Middle." It's the space in between zero and a hundred percent—the 1 percent to 99 that's not quite there yet, or not far away from the start of your journey.

That space in between doing nothing and achieving your goal is where all the failure, risk, defeat, and potential ridicule happen. If you don't try, you believe you're safe from those things. By reaching your goal, however, you're also immune from rejection or ridicule because you've already won. But everything in between allows for all your fears to manifest.

We're compelled to keep watching movies and reading books because the stakes are high. Just when the hero is about to win, tragedy or failure strikes. We, as the viewer, are then forced to know how it's all going to work out. The tension, failure, and struggle all keep us turning pages. Without these chapters, we could not be convinced of an epic ending or moments of victory because (let's be honest) that's not how real life works.

It's important to remember that just like a story has chapters, our own lives have these chapters. What we do in these chapters of our lives determines whether—like our heroes—we face ridicule and failure and step into the Courageous Middle or whether we continue to stand on the sidelines believing in a false immunity from the things we fear, while we never grow stronger.

In your battle against depression you'll have bad days. But you'll also have good days. What you do in between is what matters. Stepping into the Courageous Middle will ensure there's progress as opposed to stagnation.

But perhaps you're wondering just how to take that step.

The bravest step you can take every day is the one that keeps you going. So take that messy, imperfect, seemingly insignificant one. Starting is victory. Continuing is victory.

The more you put one foot in front of the other, however imperfect, moves you further from zero and off the barren planet of depression.

And that's courageous.

It's good to understand the thought patterns or your excuses that your mind defaults to because when you notice yourself saying those same things, you can practice developing resilience and optimism by choosing a different response when you feel your knee jerk to keep you safe at 0 percent or 100 percent instead of pushing into the 1 to 99 percent.

What can you tell yourself instead when you feel yourself knee jerking to those excuses?

What would help get you off the starting line and stepping into the Courageous Middle?

GETTING YOU BACK IN ORBIT

The year is 2330. Mankind has cultivated the Moon, but its inhabitants rebel and threaten Earth with thermonuclear war. The countries on Earth band together to fight their lunar inhabitants and choose to destroy the Moon.

The results are cataclysmic.

Losing the Moon causes famine because of changes in the tides and debris slamming into cities throughout the world. Worst of all, the Earth loses its gravitational axis and our orbit around the sun becomes unstable causing more famine and plague. Mankind plunges into chaos.

In this hypothetical situation we see just how much one situation can affect all aspects of humanity. In the same respect, depression can have unintended effects on your life and toss you out of orbit. This is why it's important to take the whole person and their situations into consideration before you act.

If you haven't noticed by now, each chapter explores aspects of the whole person—spiritually, emotionally, relationally, physically, and so on. Were we to only home in on one area and say "focus on that and step into the Courageous Middle there," the unintended consequences—much like the example of destroying a rebellion on the Moon—could be dire. We could throw you out of orbit.

This is why we've focused so closely on all aspects dealing with your depression to ensure you recognize all the places underpinning your depression. We want you to explore what it would be like to be free of those things, or what a depression-free vision of your life would be like in that area.

That's the key to this book—exploring all aspects of you, not just a portion. It's having you list out potential next steps you personally find beneficial, understanding the adversity you could face, and creating plans of your own to grow stronger.

You're meant for so much more than staying trapped on a barren rock known as the dwarf planet. You're meant to explore and cultivate others. But sometimes you may find yourself revisiting that old frozen wasteland, and that's okay.

Right now you may be on Pluto wondering how you'll ever make it to Mercury so you can be close to the sun once more. What truly matters, however, is what you do to find your exit strategy off the rock and get back into orbit. Let's say that by the end of this book you've stepped off the dwarf planet, but find yourself on Neptune. It may feel as if you have such a long way to go and are just stuck on a newer planet that's still strange and somewhat cold. But here's what you need to realize—you made it to a whole new planet and are even closer to the sun than you've ever been before.

So in your journey, take moments not to look at how far you have to go, but how far you've *come*. Turn around and wave at the dwarf planet, and each time you reflect, you'll realize just how much progress you've made.

And one day when you reflect, you just might not even be able to see the dwarf planet from where you're standing.

HOLD FAST. WE BELIEVE IN YOU.

DAILY/WEEKLY EXERCISE

Like we stated, in order to heal there has to be a Whole Person Solution. Here we've created a sample wheel that shows the aspects that might be affected by your depression that we've explored in this book. As a daily or weekly reminder, you can use this wheel to explore everything from your emotions to your relationships to your physical well-being. This way you're exploring all of you and not just the parts.

I invite you to refer back to sections of this workbook and revisit exercises to walk you through areas where you may be stuck. If an aspect isn't affected, then don't mark it. Over time as you explore a whole-person approach, I hope you'll discover the strength to forge forward.

- ◼ **Aspects of a Whole Person (*Physically, Spiritually, Philosophically/existentially, Intellectually, Emotionally, Relationally and sexually*)**

- ◼ **How I feel today (*1-awful, 10-great*)**   ◻ **One task I can do today to grow**

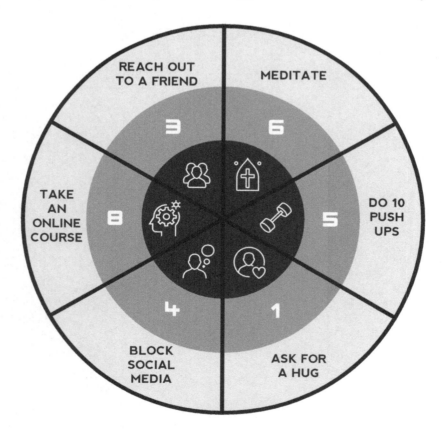

WORKS CITED

INTRODUCTION

Motivation Madness. *YouTube* interview with Chris Evans, https://www.youtube.com/watch?v=HqSoxMOrVeE.

CHAPTER 1

American College Health Association, American College Health Association–National College Health Assessment II: Reference Group Executive Summary Spring 2014. Hanover, MD: American College Health Association, 2014.

American Psychological Association (December 2015), *By the Numbers: Men and Depression*, http://www.apa.org/monitor/2015/12/numbers.aspx.

National Institute of Mental Health, *Depression*, https://www.nimh.nih.gov/health/topics/depression/index.shtml.

National Institute of Mental Health, *Major Depression*, https://www.nimh.nih.gov/health/statistics/major-depression.shtml.

National Institute of Mental Health, *Teen Depression*, https://www.nimh.nih.gov/health/publications/teen-depression/index.shtml.

World Federation for Mental Health, *DEPRESSION: A Global Crisis*. Occoquan: World Federation for Mental Health, 2015.

World Health Organization, *Depression*, http://www.who.int/en/news-room/fact-sheets/detail/depression.

CHAPTER 2

Sugarman, J., The Rise of Teen Depression, *Johns Hopkins Health Review*, Fall/Winter, 2017, 42–51.

CHAPTER 3

A special thanks to Melissa Hartwig, Co-Founder of Whole30, who reviewed this section and chose to share portions of her story with the team at HeartSupport.

Steven, C., P. Marcus and Mark Olfson, National Trends in the Treatment for Depression from 1998 to 2007, *Arch Gen Psychiatry*, 2010, 67 (12).

CHAPTER 4

MacIntyre, A., *After Virtue: A Study in Moral Theory*, Third Edition. Notre Dame, IN: University of Notre Dame Press, 2007.

Norris, K., *Acedia & Me: A Marriage, Monks, and a Writer's Life*. New York: Riverhead Books, 2010.

Pew Research Center (February 17, 2010), *Religion among the Millennials*, http://www.pewforum.org/2010/02/17/religion-among-the-millennials/.

CHAPTER 5

Easterlin, R. A., Does Economic Growth Improve the Human Lot? Some Empirical Evidence, *University of Pennsylvania*, 1974, 89–125.

Ferriss, T., *Tools of Titans: The Tactics, Routines, and Habits of Billionaires, Icons, and World-Class Performers*. New York: Houghton Mifflin Harcourt, 2016.

Jones, E., R. Woolven, B. Durodie and S. Wessely, Civilian Morale during the Second World War: Responses to Air Raids Re-examined, *Social History of Medicine*, 2004, 17(3), 463–479.

Junger, S. Why did suicide rates go down in New York after 9/11? (J. Tapper, Interviewer) CNN, May 24, 2016.

Seligman, M. E. P. *Helplessness: On Depression, Development, and Death.* San Francisco: W. H. Freeman, 1992.

CHAPTER 6

"The Sermon on the Mount" can be found in any biblical translation of the Gospel of Matthew, chapters 5 through 7.

CHAPTER 7

Covey, Stephen, "Habit 5: Seek First to Understand, Then to Be Understood," *The 7 Habits of Highly Effective People.*

CHAPTER 8

Brown, Pierce, *Red Rising Trilogy.* (I cannot recommend this series enough. I hope you read it and become as obsessed as I have.)

ACKNØWLEDGMENTS

Whew! That was a lot wasn't it?

Imagine studying depression for over eight months, writing about it almost daily, and then interviewing a lot of depressed men and women. Draining is somewhat of an understatement and I had to practice what I preached most days to ensure I didn't end up on the dwarf planet indefinitely.

At the time of writing this acknowledgment, the team at HeartSupport is in the throes of fundraising to ensure thousands of copies of this book get into the hands of those who need them most this summer. However, that would never have happened were it not for the men and women who opened their lives and shared the dark fog that too often encompasses them. Our 500 respondents were the ones who layed the groundwork, and any healing people find will directly result from their contribution to this book.

As no book is complete without the efforts of multiple people besides the author, these are the people I want to thank:

The HeartSupport Family:

Nate Hilpert—after the first pass of this book, Nate's suggestions and edits took us from talking about depression to focusing on the whole person. The workbook questions he provided made each section shine, and he was honest enough to tell me to chop off thousands of unnecessary words. As much as you hear my voice in *Dwarf Planet*, you'll hear his. Jake Luhrs—his friendship and faith continue to inspire and push me further in my writing than ever before while giving me the space to test risky waters. The rest of the team at HeartSupport— Casey, Dan, John, our Board of Directors, amazing volunteers, and our faithful donors. I can't thank you enough for empowering life transformation.

To my friends and family:

My editor, Sandra Wendel, knows what I'm trying to say and has the guts to tell me when I'm unclear. Working with her now on two books has been a delight. True to her craft, she's encouraging but intent on slaughtering words to make them rise from the ashes. I couldn't ask for a better wordsmith.

My good friend and National Champion Slam Poet, Andre Bradford, is the reason behind the title of this book. His poem, "Dwarf Planet," shook me to my core and after hearing it, I knew we had to collaborate. His feedback and friendship has helped to make this book a reality. Now we just have to get his poem, a presentation, and this workbook ready for schools and universities. Just a minor task, right?

My wife is—and continues to be—my rock. The way she feels deeply and can understand others' pain better than I can shaped many concepts in *Dwarf Planet.* Several stories you read are ones I ran by her. She remains my muse.

My family and friends are perhaps my greatest champions. Promoting HeartSupport's cause, my articles online, and the books I write. Thank you for your unwavering support.

Last, if you've read anything I've written online or in a book, it's clear that like the famed author C. S. Lewis, I serve the great King Aslan. This has not been without doubt, hardships, and many questions. But just like when one of Lewis's characters asks if Aslan is a safe lion, this response sums up my journey and thanks to Him:

Safe? Who said anything about safe? 'Course he isn't safe. But he's good. He's the King, I tell you.
—THE LION, THE WITCH, AND THE WARDROBE

ABOUT THE AUTHOR

Benjamin Sledge is the Executive Director for HeartSupport. Prior to joining the organization, he spent eleven years in the US Army with tours of duty in Iraq and Afghanistan. He is the recipient of a Bronze Star, Purple Heart, and two Army Commendation Medals for his actions overseas.

In addition to his role within the organization, Ben is a voracious reader and writer. He has authored several viral articles ranging from the masculinity crisis to veterans' mental health. His first love, however, is writing science fiction/fantasy where he is currently at work tearing his hair out resolving plot holes in his first fantasy trilogy. In his personal life, he hangs his hipster beanie in Austin, Texas, with his wife and daughter and does his part keeping Austin weird by adding to his collection of tattoos.

About the Medical Advisor: Dr. Michelle Saari sits on the Board of Directors for HeartSupport and has served as a mental health professional for the past fourteen years. She holds both a PhD and master's degree in psychology and is a licensed mental health provider and board-certified clinical supervisor in the state of Minnesota. She is also a Nationally Certified Counselor through the NBCC (National Board for Certified Counselors). She currently works at the Minnesota Department of Corrections where she serves as Director of Psychological Services.

As a longtime fan of the heavy metal music industry, Dr. Saari was aware of the negativity and darkness that many in the scene face. Seeing HeartSupport as a unique blend of the music community, relationship building, and hope for those struggling, she began volunteering on the ground at Vans Warped Tour. She has helped the organization grow to reach even more people while encouraging others to live the healthiest lives they can and discover their best self.

Outside of her professional service, she can be found exploring the outdoors, spending time exercising, and attending as many concerts and music festivals as her schedule allows.

ABØUT HEARTSUPPØRT

HeartSupport was created by Grammy-nominated musician Jake Luhrs of metal band August Burns Red. After seeing his fans struggling through the same issues and addictions he went through growing up, he wanted to use his platform to impact a generation.

In 2016, the organization won a Philanthropy Award in recognition of their work at the Alternative Press Music Awards. In 2017, the organization was recognized as one of the Top 100 nonprofits in the world for social innovation.

The team at HeartSupport often travels around the United States educating churches, nonprofits, and other organizations, while weaving engaging content along with statistics to inform and train their audiences regarding issues facing today's generation.

ReWrite

THE JOURNEY FROM SELF-HARM
TO HEALING

Self-Harm, Self-Injury, Cutting—Hope for a Generation,
Help for Families

Many in the emerging generation have found themselves in a hopeless cycle of self-harm. Whether it's cutting, burning, hair pulling, or beating themselves up with guilt and shame, they can't get out of the same rut. Most aren't even sure why they do it. All they know is that for some reason, it helps.

For men and women across the globe, it may seem like nothing will get better. Most believe no one understands self-harm or that real help is elusive and hard to find.

If that sounds like you, we have good news. You're not sick, crazy, or doomed to hurt yourself for the rest of your life. ReWrite will help clear up the stigmas and reasons behind self-harm, tackle the hard topics of guilt and shame, and provide the proven steps to bring you to a place of hope and healing. And if you're a concerned family member or friend, you'll finally understand what's going on and how you can help.

Join others who have successfully turned their lives around with information provided here.

Step into the journey. ReWrite your story.

Made in the USA
Middletown, DE
01 January 2019